D1373112

OUT
OF THE
BOX
DESSERTS

OUT *of the* BOX
DESSERTS

Simply Spectacular,
Semi-Homemade Sweets

HAYLEY PARKER

The Countryman Press
A division of W. W. Norton & Company
Independent Publishers Since 1923
New York   London

For information about permission to reproduce selections from this book,
write to Permissions, The Countryman Press, 500 Fifth Avenue, New York, NY 10110

For information about special discounts for bulk purchases, please contact
W. W. Norton Special Sales at specialsales@wwnorton.com or 800-233-4830

Manufacturing by Quad/Graphics, Taunton
Book design by Natalie Olsen, Kisscut Design

The Countryman Press
www.countrymanpress.com

A division of W. W. Norton & Company, Inc.
500 Fifth Avenue, New York, NY 10110
www.wwnorton.com

978-1-58157-409-8

10 9 8 7 6 5 4 3 2 1

This cookbook is dedicated to my loyal and rock-star amazing readers who have supported me since the beginning. Thank you!

CONTENTS

Introduction

Once upon a time, long, long ago (well, okay, it was 2012, but doesn't that feel like forever ago?), I decided I wanted to create a blog. All I was sure of was that it would be a place on the Internet to share fun cupcake recipes with my invisible Internet friends.

Invisible they were. For the longest time, my only readers were myself and my mom. I would stalk the page counter religiously and squeal with delight when I reached 30 visitors in one month. Despite the lack of traffic, I still continued posting recipe after recipe, complete with a story and a picture, to entice readers to my site. For a year and a half, barely anyone visited, but I was content with my space on the Internet and proud of my recipes.

Then, as cliché as it totally sounds (and is), everything changed overnight. Suddenly, I had Internet friends—people who would regularly comment on my blog, share my posts on Facebook and Twitter, and pin my recipes on Pinterest. Suddenly, I had big-name brands wanting to work with me, send me free products, and promote my recipes. Suddenly, I had this notoriety that materialized out of nowhere and I was seeing my recipes on popular websites like *Huffington Post*, *Good Morning America*, and *Ladies' Home Journal*. Even to this day, with the page counter nearing 15,000 views a day, a bunch of big-name-brand partnerships under my belt, and a cookbook, I'm still pinching myself because I can't believe it's real.

Even though several years have now passed since its conception, *The Domestic Rebel* blog has remained true to its aesthetic—using ordinary, everyday ingredients to create extraordinarily awesome desserts. I've never pretended to be a culinary genius (in fact, I took one—ONE—class in college and it was on pairing food and wine. I really only wanted to take it so I could drink wine at 9 a.m. on a Tuesday because it was *for my GRADE*) and I don't act like I know everything there is to know. The saying "baking is a science" used to scare me off for two reasons: One, because I was terrible at science in school, and two, because it made baking sound like it was some unachievable art form that only the greatest pastry chefs in the world could master. So. Not. True. Y'all.

While you can't necessarily throw a bunch of baking junk together, cross your fingers, and hope something magical will happen in the oven, and while, yes, there is *some* kind of science behind baking, that's not to say only fairies and French chefs can master desserts. This reminder, along with my simple aesthetic, is what has made *The Domestic Rebel* such a ridiculous success. It shows anyone and everyone, from the novice to the experienced, that baking can be *fun* and does not have to require abnormal ingredients, techniques, or machinery. In fact, in my eyes, baking isn't so much a science as it is an (achievable) art form. We're baking our feelings; we're baking for our loved ones; we're baking to challenge ourselves, to try new things, to satisfy cravings. We're baking because we want a dang brownie, and we want it *now,* and we want to bake it in a way that's friendly, approachable, realistic, and *easy.*

I use store-bought ingredients like cake mix and refrigerated cookie dough and transform them into outrageously awesome desserts. Take, for instance, my Chocolate Gooey Butter Cake, made with cake mix, Nutella, powdered sugar, and cream cheese. It's SO sinfully rich and delicious—you won't even know it came from a box! How about my Sinful Brookie Cake? Guests will be none the wiser when they take a bite—only you have to know it started with a roll of refrigerated cookie dough!

This book also has an entire section on my signature creation: Brownie Bombs. What's a brownie bomb? It started as an egg-free chocolate chip cookie dough ball wrapped in a baked, fudgy brownie, coated in chocolate and chocolate chips. Since its conception in 2013, I've made several other brownie bombs filled with wonderful,

unexpected surprises . . . some of which are in this book! Think Baklava Brownie Bombs—fudgy brownies surrounding crisp, sugary sweet baklava—or Cheesecake Brownie Bombs, filled with irresistible creamy cheesecake. Each one is better than the last, and I know you'll love this inventive and fun chapter!

Whatever you do, have FUN. My recipes are created to be easy and accessible but with unique twists that keep you coming back for more. I dare you to find a baking snob who frowns upon packaged ingredients and give them my Blueberry Muffin Cake, bursting with fresh blueberries and topped with a tantalizing homemade crumb. I guarantee they won't know it started with a boxed mix.

So get in the kitchen, tie on your apron, and get baking! Consider this book a talisman that guides you through your kitchen, creating unexpected new desserts with a few simple ingredients that will inspire you to think outside of the box! If you ever have any questions, you can always reach out to me on my website—I'd love to hear from you!

Happy Baking!!
XO, Hayley

Kitchen Must-Haves

In order to navigate through each chapter of this cookbook, you'll want to have some pantry staples on hand. These are essential ingredients that will save you time, money, and a huge hassle down the line. I always have my pantry stocked with these ingredients so I can bake anything at a moment's notice!

* Cake mix: Assorted flavors. I recommend having chocolate, yellow, and vanilla on hand all the time.

* Brownie mix: I use chocolate fudge brownie mixes—I think they work best when "fudge" is in the title.

* Canned frosting: Chocolate, vanilla, and cream cheese are my favorites.

* Boxed pudding mix: I always have chocolate and vanilla on hand—it's my secret ingredient for any cake or cupcake!

* Butter: Make sure it's the REAL stuff! I use unsalted so I can adjust the salt in each recipe accordingly. Use salted if you'd like, but omit the salt from the recipe.

* Large eggs

* Oil (vegetable or canola)

* Brown sugar: Light or dark, you ask? Use what you have on hand! Dark will produce a richer, deeper, more molasses flavor.

* White sugar

* Powdered sugar

* All-purpose flour

* Baking powder

* Baking soda

* Cornstarch: My secret ingredient for fluffy cookies!

* Milk or heavy cream: For frosting, glazes, and egg-free cookie dough

* Chocolate and vanilla almond bark/candy coating: This chocolate has a higher melting point and is less prone to seizing (see page xiii) when heated. You can find it in the baking aisle near the chocolate chips.

* Assorted chips: I always have semi-sweet, peanut butter, butterscotch, mini chocolate, and white chocolate chips in my cupboard.

* Sprinkles (because duh)

* Aluminum foil: It makes clean-up a cinch!

* Cooking spray: It makes your life a lot easier . . . unless you enjoy spending hours washing dishes.

* Sweetened condensed milk: Regular is best, but in a pinch, fat-free will do. Make sure you buy condensed milk and not evaporated milk—there's a big difference!

* Vanilla extract: Pure is best.

* An 8×8" pan, a 9×13" pan, two round 9" pans, 9" springform pan, two (12-cavity) cupcake pans, a Bundt pan, and baking sheets

* Silicone baking liners: They truly make clean-up and baking so simple.

* A handheld electric mixer or a stand mixer: It makes things so much easier!

* Cookie dough scoop: I buy it in tablespoon size for easy measuring.

These helpful tips and tricks will guide you through the prepping, baking, serving, and clean-up process swimmingly!

* To line pans with foil in one easy step, simply flip the pan upside-down and tear off a piece of foil that's slightly larger than the pan. Drape the foil over the bottom and sides of the pan to conform to the shape of the pan. Set the foil aside, flip the pan over, and then simply slip the foil lining into the pan. Grease with cooking spray, and you're ready to go! When serving, use the overhang of the foil to lift the treat out of the pan, then cut into squares or bars. Your pan will be clean and all you have to do is toss the foil!

* I usually recommend using softened butter, which you can achieve by letting it sit at room temperature for about 30 minutes to one hour. However, patience isn't my virtue and I like to microwave it, unwrapped, for about 15 to 20 seconds.

* When measuring dry ingredients like flour and cake mix, spoon the dry ingredient into your measuring cup until it's full, then level it off with a butter knife. For sugar and brown sugar, simply scooping it using the measuring cup is fine.

* When dipping things in chocolate—like my Brownie Bombs—simply drop the treat into the chocolate and use a fork to spoon the chocolate over the top, coating it on all sides. Then lift the treat out of the chocolate using the fork, and gently slide it off of the fork and onto a piece of foil or parchment. You can also use a toothpick to help guide the treat off of the fork's tines.

* Speaking of chocolate, whenever you are melting chocolate or almond bark, make sure all of your bowls, forks, spoons, and spatulas are free of any water residue. Even the tiniest droplet of water can cause chocolate to seize. When chocolate seizes, it thickens or hardens during the melting process and ends up turning into a dense paste, rendering the chocolate completely useless!

Sweet-Inspired Cakes and Cupcakes

Cake and Cupcake
Tips & Tricks

* Many of these recipes start off with a cake mix. I like to keep my pantry fully stocked with multiple flavors so I'm prepared whenever my inspiration strikes.

* I like buying cupcake liners that don't lose color in the baking process. You can usually find these at craft stores, baking supply stores, or online.

* For pretty decorated cupcakes, I like using disposable piping bags and metal tips. For a closed star-frosted cupcake, I like using Atecco brand #849, which is a large tip that does not need a coupler. For an open star-frosted cupcake, I like using Atecco brand #828. For a round, open tip, I like using Atecco brand #807. All of these tips can be found at craft stores, baking supply stores, or online. However, in a pinch, you can always spoon your frosting into a gallon-sized plastic bag, seal out the air, and snip off a corner of the bag to pipe.

* If your desired look is a cupcake piled high with frosting, I recommend doubling the frosting ingredients. Otherwise, smearing it on with an offset spatula will do the trick!

* Cakes are easily tested with a cake tester or toothpick inserted near the center. The toothpick should come back clean or with moist (not wet) crumbs. Cakes should be cooled completely before being frosted. Unless specified, most cakes can stand at room temperature, covered, for about 4 days.

Frosting
Tips & Tricks

* I have from-scratch frostings in this book, but I'm also a fan of using a store-bought tub. You can always substitute that when you're in a time pinch (or prefer the flavor!).

* I like using real butter in my recipes, rather than shortening or margarine. For one, butter produces a better-tasting product, and two, butter-based frosting recipes are easier to pipe onto cooled cakes, cookies, and cupcakes.

* Most of my frosting recipes are a rough estimate for ingredient measurements. If you need a really stiff frosting for piping and decorating, use more powdered sugar. If you want to cut the sweetness of your frosting, start by adding ½ teaspoon salt or even a squeeze of lemon juice.

* If you find your frosting to be too stiff, add one tablespoon of milk or heavy cream at a time until the frosting is the right consistency. If your frosting is too runny, add more powdered sugar, ½ cup at a time, until the frosting is the right consistency. For piping and spreading, I find the right consistency to be light and fluffy. When you hold the beater upside down, the frosting peaks shouldn't sag or fall quickly.

* Cream cheese-based frostings should be covered and stored in the fridge. Buttercream frostings and chocolate ganache can be stored in the fridge or at room temperature. Bring any refrigerated cupcakes to room temperature before serving.

Sinful Brookie Cake

I was never the girl who wore racy clothes to school. I wore cut-off denim Bermuda shorts that made me look like a female version of Huckleberry Finn and it was embarrassing in more ways than one. I had friends in high school who wore more body-conscious garb but hey, if that's what rocks your boat, more power to you. I'm not one to judge. The original name of this cake is actually a little risqué . . . you may have heard of it on the Internet. I changed it up because the cake is far more sinful than anything else. One bite and you'll see why! SERVES 8

INGREDIENTS

1 package (30-ounce) refrigerated chocolate chip cookie dough, room temperature

1 package Oreo cookies

1 box chocolate fudge brownie mix, plus ingredients listed in package directions

FOR TOPPING

1 cup semi-sweet chocolate chips

⅓ cup heavy whipping cream

FOR VANILLA FROSTING

½ cup (1 stick) butter, softened to room temperature

1 teaspoon vanilla extract or vanilla bean paste (see Note)

3–4 cups powdered sugar

¼ cup heavy cream or milk

NOTE: Vanilla bean paste is a highly concentrated form of vanilla extract. It has real flecks of vanilla beans in it to give it that indulgent, rich appearance and extraordinary flavor. You can find it online, but also at specialty craft and food stores.

1. Preheat oven to 350 degrees F. Liberally grease a 9" springform pan and an 8 × 8" pan with cooking spray and set aside.

2. Cut off ¼ of the cookie dough log and set aside. Press the remaining ¾ of the cookie dough into the prepared springform pan in an even layer, bringing it up the sides just a little bit. Top the cookie dough layer with a layer of Oreos, filling the space as much as possible.

3. Meanwhile, prepare the brownie batter according to package directions. Pour about ⅔ of the brownie batter into the pan over the layer of Oreos. Pour the rest of the brownie batter into the prepared 8 × 8" pan and set aside.

4. Place the layered cake into the oven and bake for approximately 40 to 50 minutes, testing the cake in the center with a toothpick at the 40-minute mark to ensure doneness. Toothpick should have moist—not wet—crumbs. Cool in the pan completely before removing the springform outer piece.

5. Shape the leftover cookie dough into cookies and as cake cools, bake the chocolate chip cookies on a greased or silicone-liner lined baking pan and bake the brownies. Cookies should take about

continued

9 to 10 minutes, and brownies should take about 15 to 20. Cool both completely before chopping into smaller, bite-size pieces, along with chopping up the remaining Oreo cookies into bite-size pieces.

6. In a medium microwave-safe bowl, melt together the semi-sweet chocolate chips and the heavy whipping cream for about 40 seconds, stirring well until smooth. Allow the ganache to set for about 5 minutes, then pour over the top of the cake, and spread to the edges. Top the center of the cake with the chopped chocolate chip cookie pieces, brownie pieces, and Oreo cookie pieces.

7. Prepare the frosting according to the recipe below and fill a disposable piping bag with it. Pipe it using an open-star tip around the edge of the cake. Store and serve the cake at room temperature. Cake can be kept covered for up to 5 days.

VANILLA FROSTING

1. In the bowl of a stand mixer, cream together butter and vanilla bean paste until creamy, about 2 minutes. Gradually add in the powdered sugar, about 1 cup at a time, until frosting is light and fluffy. Add in the cream or milk one tablespoon at a time if frosting is too thick.

Blueberry Muffin Cake

Growing up, my parents never cooked ... and I mean never. If they did, it was always something like macaroni and cheese or hot dogs, and really, that's heaven to a kid so I can't complain. One of the things we did bake? Blueberry muffins from a box. We had those all the time, and we never grew sick of them. There's something so nostalgic about blueberry muffins to me: waking up early on a Saturday morning to watch cartoons, then helping my mom stir in the can of blueberries. Ah, canned blueberries—so wrong, yet so right. Yes, canned blueberries are used in this recipe, but alongside real, fresh blueberries, too. The canned blueberries add some fun purple-y color to the batter but also that nostalgic taste we're after. The fresh blueberries add that great flavor. Watching cartoons while eating this cake? Totally optional. **SERVES 8**

INGREDIENTS

1 box blueberry muffin mix with can of blueberries, plus ingredients listed in package directions

1 teaspoon vanilla extract

1 cup fresh blueberries

⅓ cup butter, melted

½ cup brown sugar

¾ cup all-purpose flour

1 teaspoon ground cinnamon

Pinch nutmeg

FOR GLAZE

1 cup powdered sugar

1 teaspoon vanilla extract

2–3 tablespoons milk or cream

NOTE: Don't care for blueberry muffin mix? Omit the canned and fresh blueberries and throw in dried cranberries, fresh raspberries, raisins, or chocolate chips!

1. Preheat oven to 350 degrees F. Liberally grease a 9" springform pan with cooking spray, preferably baking spray with flour. Set aside.

2. In a large bowl, prepare the blueberry muffin batter according to package directions, and add the vanilla extract to the batter. Stir in the rinsed canned blueberries and the fresh blueberries and gently fold to combine. Pour the mixture evenly into the prepared pan.

3. Meanwhile, in a medium bowl, combine the melted butter, brown sugar, flour, cinnamon, and nutmeg with a fork until coarse crumbs come together. Sprinkle the crumb mixture liberally over the top of the cake batter.

4. Bake for approximately 30 to 35 minutes or until a toothpick inserted near the center comes out clean or with moist—not wet—crumbs. Cool in the pan completely and remove springform outer piece.

5. Prepare the glaze: In a small bowl, whisk together the powdered sugar, vanilla, and milk or cream until smooth and pourable. Drizzle with a spoon over the cooled cake and let the glaze set briefly, about 10 minutes. Cut cake into wedges and serve!

Chocolate Galaxy Cupcakes

The best part about being a kid at my grandma's house was the fact that she always had a huge stash of snack cakes and treats. Twinkies, crunch cakes, ding-dongs and oatmeal crème pies everywhere. All we had to do was ask politely for one and she'd give us two. Score! Or we could just sneak into the kitchen when she was watching her soap operas and snatch a couple packages while she wasn't looking. One of my favorites was the Cosmic Cupcake: a chocolate cupcake filled with a marshmallow-y center and topped with a layer of fudgy frosting and rainbow chips. It has every quality I want in a snack cake, not to mention its striking good looks. These cupcakes are easy to make and delicious. **18 CUPCAKES**

INGREDIENTS

1 box chocolate fudge cake mix

½ cup oil

1 cup buttermilk

3 eggs

1 (3.4-ounce) box instant chocolate pudding mix

FOR FILLING

1 (7-ounce) jar marshmallow fluff

1 cup vanilla frosting (page 5)

FOR CHOCOLATE FROSTING

½ cup (1 stick) butter, room temperature

½ cup cocoa powder

1 teaspoon vanilla extract

3–4 cups powdered sugar

⅓ cup heavy cream or milk

FOR TOPPING

⅔ cup rainbow chip sprinkles (see Note)

NOTE: Rainbow chip sprinkles are usually sold in craft stores such as Michael's or Jo-Ann, or in cake decorating stores. They look like mini rainbow chocolate chips but have a candy shell. If you can't find them, use other candy-coated chocolate candies or rainbow sprinkles.

1. Preheat oven to 350 degrees F. Line 18 muffin cavities with paper liners. Set aside.

2. In a large bowl, beat the chocolate fudge cake mix, oil, buttermilk, eggs, and dry pudding mix together with an electric mixer for about 2 minutes or until combined. Fill the muffin cups until about ¾ of the way full with the cake batter.

3. Bake the cupcakes for approximately 15 to 18 minutes or until a toothpick inserted near the center comes out clean or with moist—not wet—crumbs. Cool completely. Once cooled, use a sharp paring knife to core the center out of each cupcake, careful not to cut through the bottom of the cupcake. Discard the cores by eating them or bribing your children with them.

4. Meanwhile, make the filling. In a medium bowl, fold together the marshmallow fluff and vanilla frosting until combined. Spoon this fluff mixture into a large disposable piping bag, seal out the air, and snip off the tip of the bag. Pipe the filling into each cupcake center until the center is completely filled. Pop the cupcakes into the freezer for about 10 minutes.

continued

5. While the cupcakes are chilling, make the chocolate frosting. Microwave the chocolate frosting (directions follow) in a small bowl for about 20 to 30 seconds, stirring until smooth, soft, and pourable. (If you are using ready-made, you can warm it in the tub. Just remember to remove the foil cap!)

6 Remove the cupcakes from the freezer and, working quickly, dip the tops of the cupcakes into the mostly melted chocolate frosting, coating the tops of the cupcakes completely. Allow excess frosting to drip off, then sprinkle the tops of the cupcakes with the rainbow chip sprinkles. Let the chocolate set for about 15 minutes before serving.

CHOCOLATE FROSTING

1. In the bowl of a stand mixer, cream together the butter, cocoa powder, and vanilla extract. Gradually add in the powdered sugar, 1 cup at a time, until frosting is light and fluffy. If frosting is too thick, stream in some of the heavy cream.

Chocolate Gooey Butter Cake

Chocolate. Is there anything it can't do? I used to have a dear friend named Joan who loved chocolate. In fact, we met through blogging and her blog was titled *Chocolate, Chocolate and More*. That's precisely how much she loved the stuff. Any time I'd go out with Joan, she'd always have to order all of the chocolate desserts to sample each and every one of them. She'd sip on a Kahlua and cream drink while she did so, always insisting the bartender put it in a tall glass because measly glasses weren't her jam. Joan taught me to enjoy chocolate, savor every bite, and sample everything—why be indecisive when you can literally have it all? While Joan's no longer with us, her spirit lives on through me whenever I eat a piece of chocolate. When I took a bite of this cake, I knew she was telling me it was something I *had* to share with you! SERVES 8

INGREDIENTS

1 box chocolate cake mix

½ cup (1 stick) butter, melted

1 egg

FOR FILLING

1 (8-ounce) package cream cheese, room temperature

3 eggs

1 teaspoon vanilla extract

¾ cup Nutella or chocolate hazelnut spread of your choosing

½ cup (1 stick) butter, melted

1 (16-ounce) package powdered sugar

1. Preheat oven to 350 degrees F. Liberally spray a 9" springform pan with cooking spray, preferably baking spray with flour. Set aside.

2. In a large bowl, combine the cake mix, ½ cup melted butter, and one egg. Stir with a spatula or spoon until a soft dough has formed. Press the dough evenly into the prepared pan.

3. Make the filling: In another large bowl, beat together the cream cheese, 3 eggs, vanilla extract, and Nutella with a handheld mixer until blended and creamy, about 2 minutes. Add in ½ cup melted butter and the powdered sugar and beat slowly until mixture is combined. Pour the mixture evenly over the cake batter layer.

4. Bake for approximately 40 to 50 minutes, checking at the 40-minute mark for doneness. The outer edge should be set, but the center may still be slightly wiggly and gooey. You don't want to overbake your cake, so I advise pulling it out around the 50-minute mark. Cool in the pan completely and remove springform outer piece.

5. If desired, dust the top of the cake with additional powdered sugar.

Best Butter Cake

A few years ago, I got on a health kick. I avoided butter like the plague. I'd eat dry wheat toast like it was going out of style, knowing deep down, something was wrong with this picture. It was missing something, and that something was butter. I can't even tell you how many bland baked potatoes I consumed without butter or sour cream. It was a depressing couple years, needless to say. Now that the diet kick is over, I'm back to embracing butter, and there's no better way than this outrageous Butter Cake. SERVES 12

INGREDIENTS

1 box butter yellow cake mix

½ cup (1 stick) butter, room temperature

1 cup buttermilk

4 eggs

2 teaspoons butter extract, optional but recommended

1 (3.4-ounce) box instant vanilla pudding mix

FOR BUTTER SAUCE

¾ cup sugar

¼ cup (½ stick) butter, cut into cubes

3 tablespoons water

2 teaspoons vanilla extract

1 tablespoon powdered sugar, for dusting

1. Preheat oven to 350 degrees F. Liberally grease a Bundt pan with cooking spray, preferably baking spray with flour. Set aside.

2. In a large bowl, beat together the cake mix, butter, buttermilk, eggs, butter extract, and pudding mix with an electric mixer for 2 minutes, or until creamy and combined. Pour into the prepared pan and smooth into an even layer.

3. Bake for approximately 45 to 55 minutes or until a toothpick inserted near the center of the cake comes out with moist—not wet—crumbs. Cool for about 15 minutes in the pan.

4. While cake cools, make your butter sauce. In a small saucepan, melt together the sugar, butter, water, and vanilla extract over medium heat, stirring until sugar and butter have melted. Continue cooking until bubbles begin to form around the edges of the pot. Remove from heat.

5. Using a long skewer or a butter knife, poke holes all over the cake, being careful not to puncture through the bottom. Pour the butter sauce over the top of the cake, covering the holes. Let the cake cool completely in the pan, which allows the butter sauce to be absorbed into the cake.

6. Once cake is cool, invert from the pan onto a wire rack, and dust with powdered sugar.

Mint Cookie Overload Cake

Growing up, I spent a lot of time at my Grandma Marjorie and Grandpa Tom's house. They had the largest collection of toys I'd ever seen. I loved the miniature car with foot pedals. I'd ride that thing around like there was no tomorrow. One of my Grandpa Tom's favorite things were after-dinner mints . . . you know, the ones in the shiny green wrappers. Every so often, he'd slip us a mint and it was magical. To this day, my love of anything minty comes from him, and this cake is no exception! SERVES 8

FOR CAKE

1 box chocolate cake mix

1¼ cups buttermilk

½ cup oil

3 eggs

1 (3.4-ounce) box instant dry chocolate pudding mix

FOR FILLING

1 (8-ounce) package cream cheese, room temperature

½ cup sugar

1 teaspoon vanilla extract

2 teaspoons mint extract

1 (8-ounce) tub Cool Whip, thawed

2–3 drops green food coloring

10 Mint Oreos, finely chopped

FOR TOPPING

1 (16-ounce) tub chocolate frosting

1 teaspoon mint extract

12 Mint Oreos, coarsely chopped

NOTE: Store leftover cake in the fridge.

1. Preheat oven to 350 degrees F. Grease two 9" round cake pans with cooking spray. Set aside.

2. In a large bowl, beat together the cake mix, buttermilk, oil, eggs, and dry pudding mix with an electric mixer for about 2 minutes or until combined. Distribute batter evenly between the cake pans.

3. Bake for approximately 20 to 25 minutes or until a toothpick inserted near the center comes out clean or with moist—not wet—crumbs. Cool completely.

4. Once cake has cooled, make your filling. In a large bowl, beat the cream cheese, sugar, and vanilla and mint extracts with an electric mixer for about 1 minute, or until combined. Fold in the Cool Whip and green food coloring until your desired shade of mint has been achieved. Gently fold in the finely chopped Mint Oreos.

5. Place one cake layer onto a plate or stand, top-side down. Top with the filling mixture. It will seem like a lot, but you want this layer to be thick! Spread it out to the edges as evenly as possible. Top with the remaining cake layer, top-side up.

6. For the topping, remove the lid and foil from the tub of frosting and microwave for 20 to 30 seconds, stirring until smooth and pourable. Stir in the mint extract and pour over the top of the cake, allowing it to drip down the sides. Let sit for about 1 to 2 minutes before topping the center of the cake with the coarsely chopped Mint Oreos. Serve immediately.

Hot Fudge Sundae Cupcakes

Hot fudge sundaes were one of my favorite things as a kid. I remember requesting them from the fast food drive-thru any time we'd eat out, because let's face it: when is a hot fudge sundae *not* awesome? There's something so outrageously tempting about smooth and creamy vanilla ice cream, the thick and rich hot fudge sauce, the fun burst of color from the rainbow sprinkles, and of course, the infamous cherry on top. While I was perfectly content with my fast food sundaes, sometimes my parents would take me and my siblings out to an actual ice cream parlor, where the sundaes were ten times bigger (and ten times tastier). All that's missing from this cupcake is a spoon, but I recommend eating it faster than a spoon can allow. **18 CUPCAKES**

INGREDIENTS

1 box chocolate cake mix

1½ cups water

½ cup oil

3 eggs

1 (3.4-ounce) box dry instant chocolate
  pudding mix

FOR TOPPING

1–2 batches Vanilla Frosting (page 5)

1 (12-ounce) jar hot fudge sundae sauce,
  warmed (see Note)

Rainbow sprinkles

Maraschino cherries

NOTE: To make it easier to drizzle the hot fudge, spoon the smooth fudge into a sandwich bag, seal out the air, snip off the tip, and drizzle!

1. Preheat oven to 350 degrees F. Line 18 muffin cavities with paper liners. Set aside.

2. In a large bowl, beat together the cake mix, water, oil, eggs, and dry pudding mix with an electric mixer for 2 minutes, or until creamy and combined. Distribute evenly among the muffin cups, filling until about ¾ full.

3. Bake for approximately 15 to 18 minutes, or until a toothpick inserted near the center comes out clean or with moist—not wet—crumbs. Cool completely.

4. For the topping, spread or pipe Vanilla Frosting onto cooled cupcakes. If piping, you may want to double the batch of frosting. Drizzle with hot fudge sauce. Garnish with sprinkles and adorn the top of each cupcake with a cherry.

Red Velvet Cheesecake Swirl Cake

I used to work in a cupcake shop, and our most popular flavor by far was red velvet. One time, I had to work on Valentine's Day, our busiest day ever. There was a line wrapped around outside all for . . . red velvet cupcakes. Are you sensing my disappointment? Okay, so admittedly red velvet isn't my favorite, and that's okay—the world will continue to orbit without my love for the stuff. When you throw anything cream cheese into the mix, I instantly become a supporter. This cake has a sweet little cheesecake ribbon swirled throughout and a thick cream cheese glaze. Shh, don't tell the cupcake shop, but I like this version better. SERVES 12

INGREDIENTS

1 box red velvet cake mix

1 cup buttermilk

½ cup oil

4 eggs

1 (3.4-ounce) box dry instant cheesecake pudding mix

FOR CHEESECAKE SWIRL

4 ounces cream cheese, room temperature

½ cup sugar

1 teaspoon vanilla extract

1 egg

FOR TOPPING

1 (16-ounce) tub cream cheese frosting

Red sugar sprinkles

1. Preheat oven to 350 degrees F. Liberally grease a Bundt pan with cooking spray, preferably baking spray with flour. Set aside.

2. In a large bowl, beat the cake mix, buttermilk, oil, eggs, and dry pudding mix with an electric mixer for 2 minutes, until creamy and combined. Pour half of the batter into the prepared pan.

3. Meanwhile, make the cheesecake swirl. In a medium bowl, beat together the cream cheese, sugar, vanilla, and egg with an electric mixer for about 1 minute or until combined. Pour the cheesecake mixture into the center of the batter in the pan, avoiding touching the sides if possible. Top with the remaining red velvet cake batter.

4. Bake for approximately 40 to 50 minutes or until a toothpick inserted near the center comes out clean or with moist—not wet—crumbs. Cool in the pan completely before inverting onto a wire rack.

5. For the topping, remove the lid and foil from the tub of cream cheese icing and microwave in 10-second intervals, stirring after each interval, until pourable. Pour the frosting over the cooled cake and top with the red sprinkles.

Swiss Roll Cake

I've spent so much of my life eating snack cakes that you'd *think* I knew them all by heart and could separate my Ho-Hos from my Ding-Dongs and so forth. One terrible day a few years ago, I posted a recipe on my blog for "Ding Dong Bat Pops": little cylindrical pops that looked like bats for Halloween. People started emailing me to inform me that those were, in fact, Ho-Hos, or Swiss Rolls, as they're sometimes called. So here's this recipe out in the world forever that's completely mislabeled. It's almost as embarrassing as the time I offered to climb into a garbage can for thirty seconds in front of my crush for a dare. Almost. SERVES 8

INGREDIENTS

1 box chocolate fudge cake mix

1½ cups buttermilk

½ cup oil

3 eggs

1 (3.4-ounce) box dry instant chocolate pudding mix

FOR FILLING

1 (16-ounce) can vanilla frosting

1 (7-ounce) jar marshmallow fluff

FOR TOPPING

1 (16-ounce) tub chocolate frosting

4 Swiss Rolls, unwrapped and each cut into 5 equal slices

1. Preheat oven to 350 degrees F. Liberally grease two 9" round cake pans with cooking spray, preferably baking spray with flour. Set aside.

2. In a large bowl, beat together the cake mix, buttermilk, oil, eggs, and dry pudding mix with an electric mixer for about 2 minutes or until combined. Distribute evenly between the baking pans.

3. Bake for approximately 20 to 25 minutes or until a toothpick inserted near the center comes out dry or with moist—not wet—crumbs. Cool completely in pans before inverting to wire racks.

4. In a medium bowl, fold together the vanilla frosting and the marshmallow fluff until combined. Place one cake, flat-side up, onto a cake stand or serving platter. Spread with the marshmallow mixture in an even layer. Top with the remaining cake layer, flat-side up. Fill in any gaps between the cake layers with more marshmallow mixture.

5. Microwave frosting for about 30 to 40 seconds, stirring well, until smooth and pourable. Pour over the top of the cake, allowing the frosting to drip down the sides. Before it sets, arrange the Swiss Roll slices around the perimeter of the cake. Let the frosting set, then serve.

Chocolate Peanut Candy Cupcakes

In high school I had the worst diet. I'd eat a package of chocolate-frosted donuts every day for breakfast and for lunch I'd snack on a Snickers bar and a soda. You know, total brain food for a growing mind. There was something so enticing and satisfying about a Snickers bar. Caramel, nougat, and peanuts are my kind of party, and I always looked forward to my daily "lunch." These cupcakes remind me of those innocent high school days when I could get away with eating candy bars for lunch. **18 CUPCAKES**

INGREDIENTS

1 box chocolate fudge cake mix

½ cup oil

1 cup water

3 eggs

1 (3.4-ounce) box instant chocolate pudding mix

FOR PEANUT BUTTER FROSTING

½ cup (1 stick) butter, room temperature

½ cup creamy peanut butter

1 teaspoon vanilla extract

3–4 cups powdered sugar

¼ cup heavy cream or milk (may not use all of it)

FOR TOPPING

½ (12-ounce) jar caramel sauce

8–10 fun-size Snickers bars, chopped into bite-size pieces

1. Preheat oven to 350 degrees F. Line 18 muffin cavities with paper liners. Set aside.

2. In a large bowl, beat together the chocolate fudge cake mix, oil, water, eggs, and dry pudding mix with an electric mixer for about 2 minutes or until combined. Distribute evenly among the muffin cups, filling until about ¾ full.

3. Bake for approximately 15 to 18 minutes or until a toothpick inserted near the center comes out with moist—not wet—crumbs. Cool completely.

4. Make the frosting (directions follow). Spoon it into a disposable piping bag attached with an open-star tip. Pipe the frosting onto the cooled cupcakes. Drizzle the tops of the cupcakes with the caramel sauce, then top with a few pieces of chopped Snickers bars. Serve!

PEANUT BUTTER FROSTING

1. In the bowl of a stand mixer, cream together the butter, peanut butter, and vanilla until smooth and creamy, about 2 minutes. Add in the powdered sugar, 1 cup at a time, until frosting is light and fluffy. If frosting is too thick, add in one tablespoon of cream at a time to soften.

Snickerdoodle Sheet Cake

One of the first recipes I shared on my blog was a recipe for snickerdoodle cake. The pictures are atrocious. You live and you learn, right? I learned not to photograph food with flash, on my ugly kitchen counters, or at 6 o'clock at night. Things I've also learned not to do: run up to every dog I see while squealing; eat more than two scoops of ice cream unless I want to suffer the wrath of heart burn; and wear the color coral under any circumstance. Now I've updated my snickerdoodle cake recipe to be a sheet cake with classic sheet cake frosting (minus the cocoa and nuts . . . though I'm not morally opposed if you decide to add them!). **SERVES 24**

INGREDIENTS

1 box white cake mix

1 cup buttermilk

3 eggs

½ cup oil

1 (3.4-ounce) box instant dry vanilla pudding mix

1 teaspoon ground cinnamon

FOR VANILLA SHEET CAKE FROSTING

½ cup (1 stick) butter

¼ cup heavy cream

¼ cup brown sugar

1 teaspoon vanilla

1 teaspoon ground cinnamon

4 cups powdered sugar

FOR TOPPING

1 teaspoon ground cinnamon

½ cup sugar

NOTE: If you'd like to make this a chocolate sheet cake frosting, simply add ¼ cup cocoa powder into the saucepan and increase the heavy cream to ⅓ cup. You may also stir in chopped nuts at the end if you'd like.

1. Preheat oven to 350 degrees F. Liberally grease a 15×10" rimmed baking sheet pan with cooking spray. Set aside.

2. In a large bowl, beat the cake mix, buttermilk, eggs, oil, and dry pudding mix with an electric mixer for two minutes or until blended. Stir in one teaspoon ground cinnamon.

3. Pour the batter into the prepared pan and bake for approximately 20 to 25 minutes or until a toothpick inserted near the center comes out clean or with moist—not wet—crumbs. Cool for about 15 minutes.

4. Meanwhile, prepare the frosting (recipe below), then pour over the entire still-warm cake and spread out evenly.

5. Whisk together cinnamon and sugar, and sprinkle mixture liberally on frosted cake. Allow to set until cooled completely, about 30 to 45 minutes. Cut into squares and serve!

VANILLA SHEET CAKE FROSTING

1. In a medium saucepan, bring the butter, heavy cream, and brown sugar to a boil over medium heat. Once boiling, remove from heat and stir in the vanilla, ground cinnamon, and powdered sugar, about a cup at a time, until frosting is thick and glossy.

Piña Colada Cupcakes

When I was younger and we'd go out to restaurants as a family, my parents would sometimes order drinks from the bar. These drinks always looked so colorful and fruity, and may or may not have had a paper umbrella garnish. One day I ordered a virgin piña colada and the rest was history. I was hooked and felt so cool drinking something fancy from the bar. Nowadays I order it boozed up, but it still reminds me of the time when I thought I was cool enough to order at the bar. Ah, memories. **18 CUPCAKES**

INGREDIENTS

1 box pineapple cake mix

1 cup water

½ cup oil

3 eggs

1 (3.4-ounce) box instant dry coconut pudding mix

1 (8-ounce) can crushed pineapple, drained

FOR PINEAPPLE CREAM CHEESE FROSTING

¼ cup (½ stick) butter, room temperature

1 (8-ounce) package pineapple cream cheese, room temperature

1 teaspoon vanilla extract

1 teaspoon coconut extract (optional)

4–5 cups powdered sugar

¼ cup heavy cream or milk

FOR TOPPING

½ cup flaked coconut, toasted (see Note)

NOTE: To toast coconut, place in a single layer onto a baking sheet or small pan. Toast at 300 degrees F for about 5 minutes. Stir, then toast for another 3 minutes. Stir again, then toast for another 2 to 3 minutes or until golden brown and fragrant. Stay close, because coconut burns very easily!

1. Preheat oven to 350 degrees F. Line 18 muffin cavities with paper liners. Set aside.

2. In a large bowl, beat the cake mix, water, oil, eggs, and dry pudding mix with an electric mixer for about 2 minutes or until blended. Stir in the crushed pineapple by hand until blended.

3. Distribute batter evenly among muffin cups, filling until about ¾ full. Bake for approximately 15 to 18 minutes or until a toothpick inserted near the center comes out clean or with moist—not wet—crumbs. Cool completely.

4. Prepare Pineapple Cream Cheese Frosting according to recipe below. If piping, you may want to make two batches. Pipe or spread frosting onto the cooled cupcakes and garnish with the toasted coconut. Store covered in the refrigerator.

PINEAPPLE CREAM CHEESE FROSTING

1. In the bowl of a stand mixer, cream together the butter, cream cheese, vanilla extract, and coconut extract, if using, until smooth and creamy, about 2 minutes. Gradually add in the powdered sugar, 1 cup at a time, until frosting is light and fluffy. Add 1 tablespoon of milk or cream at a time if frosting is too thick.

Hummingbird Cupcakes

Before writing this book, I'd never had Hummingbird Cake, but I'd always wanted to have a slice. What's not to love about a spice cake filled with banana, pineapple, and pecans? It's tropical and reminds me of the time I went to the Bahamas and ordered coconut water straight from the coconut, envisioning a refreshing drink that tasted like, well, coconut. I got a coconut with slightly bitter water inside that tasted nothing like half of a piña colada. Thankfully, it didn't taint my love for coconut. If you're not a coconut fan, feel free to leave it out, but it adds the perfect sweet nuttiness atop these festive cupcakes. **18 CUPCAKES**

INGREDIENTS

1 box spice cake mix

1¼ cups buttermilk

½ cup oil

3 eggs

1 medium ripe banana, mashed (½ cup)

1 (3.4-ounce) small box dry instant banana pudding mix

1 (8-ounce) can crushed pineapple

1 cup chopped pecans

FOR TOPPING

Pineapple Cream Cheese Frosting (page 31)

1 cup flaked coconut, toasted

Mini candy-coated chocolate eggs for garnish, optional

NOTE: To toast coconut, preheat oven to 300 degrees F. Place in a single layer on a baking sheet and bake for 5 minutes. Stir, then bake for another 3 to 5 minutes. Stir once more, baking for a remaining 2 to 3 minutes or until fragrant and golden.

1. Preheat oven to 350 degrees F. Line 18 muffin cavities with paper liners. Set aside.

2. In a large bowl, beat together the cake mix, buttermilk, oil, eggs, banana, and pudding mix with an electric mixer for about 2 minutes or until blended. Stir in the crushed pineapple and pecans to combine.

3. Distribute the batter evenly among the muffin cups, filling until about ¾ full. Bake for approximately 15 to 18 minutes or until a toothpick inserted near the center comes out clean or with moist—not wet—crumbs. Cool completely.

4. Pipe or spread the Pineapple Cream Cheese Frosting onto the cooled cupcakes. If piping the frosting, make two batches of frosting. Top with a heaping tablespoon of the toasted coconut, forming a nest shape. Fill the nest with a few of the chocolate egg candies.

Best Banana Cake

Grocery shopping has always been—and still is—one of my favorite things to do. I love making a store list, clipping corresponding coupons, and making the trek to the grocery store. I think I started loving it when I was younger because the grocery store sold this frozen banana cake with banana frosting. Any time we'd shop there, I'd beg my mom to buy the cake because bananas are my jam and that cake had secret addictive qualities, kind of like Girl Scout cookies or online shopping. Nine times out of ten, she'd oblige. Here, I've recreated that cake and I have to say, this version is ten times better. SERVES 15

INGREDIENTS

1 box yellow cake mix

½ cup brown sugar

1 teaspoon ground cinnamon

2–3 ripe bananas, mashed (1 cup)

1 cup water

½ cup oil

3 eggs

2 teaspoons banana extract, optional

FOR BANANA FROSTING

¼ cup (½ stick) butter, room temperature

1 ripe banana, mashed (½ cup)

1 teaspoon vanilla extract

1–2 teaspoons banana extract, optional

1 teaspoon lemon juice

3 cups powdered sugar

1. Preheat oven to 350 degrees F. Liberally grease a 9 × 13" baking pan with cooking spray. Set aside.

2. In a large bowl, beat the cake mix, brown sugar, cinnamon, bananas, water, oil, eggs, and banana extract (if using) together with an electric mixer for 2 minutes or until blended and smooth. Pour the batter into the prepared pan.

3. Bake for approximately 30 to 35 minutes or until a toothpick inserted near the center comes out clean or with moist—not wet—crumbs. Cool completely.

4. Prepare the Banana Frosting according to recipe below and spread evenly onto the cooled cake. Refrigerate for about 30 minutes to set the frosting before cutting into squares.

BANANA FROSTING

1. In the bowl of a stand mixer, beat together the butter and mashed banana until creamy and smooth, about 1 minute. Add in the vanilla extract, banana extract (if using), and lemon juice, and beat to combine. Lastly, add in the powdered sugar, 1 cup at a time, until frosting is light, fluffy, and spreadable.

Grandma Marjorie's Coffee Cake

My Grandma Marjorie was awesome, and I remember her house being an endless inspiration of wonder and amazement. To say she was a collector would be an understatement—the woman held onto everything. As a kid, I found that to be great resource to fuel my imagination, playing with her figurines, old dolls, and dried macaroni from the 1980s (don't ask—I was a creative child and macaroni was very entertaining). Grandma Marjorie made a mean coffee cake with buttery crumbs, and a brown sugary cake with just the right amount of sweetness and love. I've adapted her recipe just a little to add more of that glorious crumb, but the basic infrastructure of the recipe remains. Miss you, Grandma! SERVES 15

INGREDIENTS

3 cups all-purpose flour

1¼ cups sugar

1¼ cups brown sugar

1½ teaspoons baking soda

1½ teaspoons baking powder

1½ teaspoons nutmeg

2 teaspoons cinnamon

½ teaspoon salt

1 cup oil

1 egg, beaten lightly

1¼ cups buttermilk

1 teaspoon vanilla extract

1. Preheat oven to 350 degrees F. Liberally grease a 9×13" baking pan with cooking spray. Set aside.

2. In a large bowl, whisk together the flour, sugar, brown sugar, baking soda, baking powder, nutmeg, cinnamon, and salt until blended. Stir in the oil until moistened and reserve 2 cups of the mixture in a separate bowl.

3. To the original bowl, add the beaten egg, buttermilk, and vanilla and stir until combined. Batter may be lumpy; this is okay. You don't want to over-mix it.

4. Pour the batter into the prepared pan and liberally sprinkle the crumb mixture over the batter as evenly as possible. Bake for approximately 30 to 35 minutes or until a toothpick inserted near the center comes out clean or with moist crumbs. Cool for about 10 minutes before cutting into squares.

New Year's Day Mimosa Pound Cake

January is a big celebration month for my family: It's the beginning of a new year, my sister Chloe's birthday, my Grammie Pat's birthday, and my birthday, all one week apart from each other. Even if we wanted to make a resolution to diet, we couldn't. Because we're celebrating almost a birthday a week, I'm usually imbibing quite a bit, and one of the drinks we make at home is a simple but delicious one: the mimosa. The delightful combination of tart orange juice and fizzy champagne can't be beat, and it stars in this buttery, luscious pound cake. SERVES 8

INGREDIENTS

½ cup (1 stick) butter, room temperature

1 cup sugar

2 eggs

2 tablespoons triple sec or orange juice

Zest of 1 orange, divided

1 teaspoon orange extract

1½ cups all-purpose flour

1 teaspoon baking powder

½ teaspoon salt

¾ cup buttermilk

FOR CHAMPAGNE GLAZE

1½ cups powdered sugar

2–3 tablespoons champagne

Reserved orange zest

1 tablespoon orange juice

NOTE: Want to skip the champagne? Simply add more orange juice to the glaze mixture.

1. Preheat oven to 350 degrees F. Liberally grease an 8" or 9" loaf pan with cooking spray, preferably baking spray with flour. Set aside.

2. In a large bowl, cream together the butter and sugar until blended, about 2 minutes. Add in the eggs, one at a time, then the triple sec, about ¾ of the orange zest, and orange extract. In a smaller bowl, whisk together the flour, baking powder, and salt.

3. Gradually add half of the flour mixture into the wet mixture, mixing well. Stream in half of the buttermilk, then alternate with the flour again and the remaining buttermilk until completely blended and smooth.

4. Pour the batter into the prepared pan and bake for approximately 40 to 50 minutes or until the top is light golden brown and a toothpick inserted near the center comes out clean or with moist crumbs. Cool in the pan completely.

5. To make the glaze, in a medium bowl, whisk together the glaze ingredients until smooth. Pour the glaze over the top and allow it to set, about 15 minutes, before cutting into slices to serve.

Molten Lava Cakes

Is there anything sexier than chocolate? Well, maybe a house cleaned by your spouse. Or your celebrity crush surprising you with a dozen red roses. Or lobster mac & cheese. No matter how you celebrate, there's something so decadent about chocolate. Whether you're single or taken, everyone can appreciate these Molten Lava Cakes. They are so simple to prepare and the recipe makes enough for seconds . . . or thirds, if you're happily single like me. Garnish with raspberries and powdered sugar and serve with ice cream. 4–6 MINI CAKES

INGREDIENTS

6 ounces semi-sweet chocolate, chopped

½ cup (1 stick) butter

1 cup powdered sugar

2 eggs

2 egg yolks

1 teaspoon vanilla extract

½ cup all-purpose flour

1. Preheat oven to 425 degrees F. Liberally grease 4 to 6 ramekins with cooking spray, preferably baking spray with flour. Depending on the size of your ramekins, you may get anywhere from 4 to 6 cakes. My ramekins are standard size (about 3") so the recipe yields 6 cakes.

2. In a large microwave-safe bowl, melt the chopped chocolate and the butter together on HIGH power for about 45 seconds. Stir, then heat for an additional 30 seconds if needed, until smooth and glossy. Add in the powdered sugar, eggs, egg yolks, vanilla extract, and flour, and stir until combined.

3. Evenly distribute the batter among the ramekins and place the ramekins on a rimmed baking sheet. Bake for approximately 13 to 15 minutes or until the cakes appear set. Let cool for about 5 minutes before gently running a butter knife around the edge of the cakes. Carefully invert each ramekin onto a plate. Heed caution, as the ramekin will still be hot.

4. Serve immediately.

Lemon Coconut Cake

This cake is easily one of my new favorites! Lemon cake is just so reminiscent of springtime, and who can resist a light and tender cake bursting with fresh citrusy flavor? Don't even get me started on the coconut frosting. It. Is. Phenomenal. Light as a cloud, super fluffy, and loaded with coconutty goodness. Paired together, the two make quite a team! SERVES 8–10

INGREDIENTS

1 box lemon cake mix

4 egg whites

1¼ cups water

½ cup unsweetened applesauce

1 (3.4-ounce) box instant lemon pudding mix

Zest of one lemon

FOR COCONUT FROSTING

1 (3.4-ounce) box instant coconut pudding mix

⅓ cup powdered sugar

1 cup cold milk

4 ounces cream cheese, room temperature

1 (8-ounce) tub Cool Whip, thawed

FOR TOPPING

1 cup shredded coconut

1 Preheat oven to 350 degrees F. Liberally grease two 9" cake pans with cooking spray and set aside.

2 In a large bowl, beat together the cake mix, egg whites, water, applesauce, lemon pudding mix, and lemon zest with an electric mixer until combined. Portion the batter evenly among the two greased cake pans and bake for approximately 18 to 20 minutes, or until the cakes spring back lightly when touched and a toothpick inserted near the center comes out mostly clean. Allow the cakes to cool in the pan for about 15 minutes before gently inverting them onto wire racks to cool completely. Prepare frosting.

3 Place a cake round on a serving platter or cake stand. Top with half of the frosting mixture, spreading it just to the border—don't actually spread to the border or else it'll all mush out. Top with the second cake and frost the top. Generously pat on the shredded coconut.

COCONUT FROSTING

1. In the bowl of a stand mixer, combine the coconut pudding, powdered sugar, and milk, and whisk until smooth. Stir in the cream cheese until combined. Fold in the Cool Whip by hand until fully incorporated. Refrigerate if not using immediately.

Strawberry Milkshake Cupcakes

There's a story in our family that my dad would always buy my mom strawberry milkshakes whenever they'd go to a burger joint. My mom had never actually said she liked strawberry milkshakes, but he had the idea in his head that she liked them. I do know that my mom loves cupcakes and she also loves strawberries, so naturally, I figured she'd like these cupcakes despite the name. She did! For those of us who do like strawberry milkshakes, these cupcakes are a dream come true! **18 CUPCAKES**

INGREDIENTS

1 box strawberry cake mix

1¼ cups buttermilk

½ cup oil

3 eggs

1 (3.4-ounce) box dry instant strawberry pudding mix

⅓ cup strawberry milk drink mix (such as Nesquik)

FOR STRAWBERRY MILKSHAKE FROSTING

½ cup (1 stick) butter, room temperature

1 teaspoon vanilla extract

¼ cup strawberry milk powder (such as Nesquik)

3½–4 cups powdered sugar

¼ cup heavy cream or milk (may not use all of it)

FOR TOPPING

18 strawberry candies or pink gumballs for decoration, optional

NOTE: This frosting isn't just awesome for Strawberry Milkshake Cupcakes—it'd also be great on lemon cupcakes, sugar cookies, or spread on fudgy brownies.

1. Preheat the oven to 350 degrees F. Line 18 muffin cavities with paper liners. Set aside.

2. In a large bowl, beat the cake mix, buttermilk, oil, eggs, dry pudding mix, and strawberry milk drink mix together with an electric mixer for about 2 minutes or until blended. Distribute the batter evenly among the muffin cups, filling until about ¾ full.

3. Bake for approximately 15 to 18 minutes or until a toothpick inserted near the center comes out clean or with moist—not wet—crumbs. Cool completely.

4. Make Strawberry Milkshake Frosting according to recipe below and spread or pipe the frosting onto the cooled cupcakes. If piping the frosting, you may want to prepare 2 batches of frosting. Garnish with strawberry candies or pink gumballs, then serve.

STRAWBERRY MILKSHAKE FROSTING

1. In the bowl of a stand mixer, cream together the butter, vanilla extract, and strawberry milk powder together until creamy and smooth, about 2 minutes. Gradually add in the powdered sugar, about 1 cup at a time, until frosting is light and fluffy. Add in the cream or milk one tablespoon at a time if frosting is too thick.

Texas Sheet Cake Bites

I don't mind living in California, but I loathe our hot weather in the summertime. The temperature often rises above 100 degrees, making it miserable for everything and everyone. This recipe came to me when it was particularly toasty outside but I was craving sheet cake—you know, with that glorious poured frosting, fudgy chocolate cake, and crunchy pecans? By using prepared brownie bites, you can bypass the whole baking thing and have your cake in no time. **30 BITES**

INGREDIENTS

30 prepared brownie bites

FOR TOPPING

½ cup (1 stick) butter

5 tablespoons cocoa powder

5 tablespoons heavy cream

4 cups powdered sugar, plus more for dusting

1 teaspoon vanilla extract

1 cup chopped pecans

1. Line a large rimmed baking sheet with foil and place the brownie bites on the sheet in a single layer. Set aside.

2. Make the topping: In a large saucepan, melt the butter with the cocoa powder and heavy cream over medium-high heat, stirring occasionally, until smooth. Bring the mixture to a boil, then immediately remove from the heat. Stir in the powdered sugar 1 cup at a time and the vanilla until combined. Fold in the pecans.

3. Drop rounded tablespoons of frosting on top of each brownie bite. Work quickly, as the sheet cake frosting tends to set quite fast. If the frosting begins to set, just put it back on the heat and stir until smooth again.

4. Allow sheet cake frosting to set for about 15 minutes before serving. Dust with powdered sugar, if you'd like.

Brownies, Blondies, and Bars
Tips & Tricks

∗ I primarily bake my bar recipes in 9×13", 8×8", or 9×9" baking pans. Each recipe will specify which pan to use.

∗ I highly recommend lining your pans with foil. Not only does this make clean-up a breeze, but it also ensures the bottom layer of the bars don't stick to the pan. Plus, if you use extra aluminum foil, you can create an overhang or "handles" for your bars to easily lift out of the pan!

∗ Most blondie, brownie, and bar recipes require a toothpick test—that is, the toothpick inserted near the center comes out clean or with moist (not wet) crumbs. However, some of the recipes will appear jiggly in the middle still. This is okay! Some bar recipes need time to set and solidify after they've baked, which is why I recommend pulling them out while they're still a little soft in the middle.

2

Brownies, Blondies, and More
Sticky, Gooey Bars

Sticky Toffee Pudding Blondies

A few years ago, I attended a conference at the Disneyland Resort. I was so pumped to learn about food blogging and sit in a conference room all day! JUST kidding. Instead, I spent 99 percent of the time on rides and stuffing myself senseless with churros and beignets. My friend Elizabeth was there and she started telling me about sticky toffee pudding. I have never had sticky toffee pudding, but I instantly became inspired to make something with that flavor profile. Behold, Sticky Toffee Pudding Blondies! They remind me of the time I completely ditched a conference in favor of riding roller coasters. Because let's be honest, roller coasters always win. **15 BARS**

INGREDIENTS

1 cup (2 sticks) butter

1 cup brown sugar

2 eggs

1 tablespoon vanilla extract

2 cups all-purpose flour

1 teaspoon baking soda

½ teaspoon salt

½ cup pitted dates, roughly chopped

½ cup toffee bits

FOR TOPPING

Caramel sauce, for drizzling over top

1. Preheat oven to 350 degrees F. Liberally grease a 9×13" baking pan with cooking spray. Set aside.

2. Melt the butter in a large saucepan over medium heat, stirring to prevent burning. Let cool for about 5 minutes. Stir in the brown sugar, then one egg at a time, and then the vanilla. Lastly, stir in the flour, baking soda, and salt until combined. Fold in the chopped dates and toffee bits.

3. Spread the batter evenly into the prepared pan and bake for approximately 20 to 25 minutes or until a toothpick inserted near the center comes out clean. Cool in the pan completely.

4. Once cooled, cut into squares and drizzle with caramel sauce. These taste great warm with ice cream, too!

Easy Cake Mix Bars

Few things in life are easy, and I learned that the hard way. A couple of things that *are* easy: smiling at a happy dog; wolfing down a bag of potato chips while binge-watching your favorite TV show; and these Cake Mix Bars. In fact, when I taught myself how to bake many years ago, these were one of the first things I baked for my family and I've never looked back. Sure, you could make a blondie from scratch—and I do have those recipes in this book! Sometimes, though, you just want something foolproof, simple, and no fuss. These bars can be customized—throw in any nut, chip, or candy you'd like! **15 BARS**

INGREDIENTS

1 box cake mix (any flavor)
2 eggs
½ cup oil
1 teaspoon vanilla extract
1 cup white chocolate chips
1 cup M&M's candies

1. Preheat your oven to 350 degrees F. Line a 9×13" pan with foil, allowing the foil to hang over the sides of the pan. Spray the foil with cooking spray. Set aside.

2. In a large bowl, combine the cake mix, eggs, oil, and vanilla extract with a spoon or spatula until a soft dough forms. Fold in the white chocolate chips and M&M's (or any other add-in you'd prefer).

3. Spread the batter into the prepared pan and bake for approximately 15 to 20 minutes or until the top is golden brown and set. Cool completely in the pan before cutting into bars.

Chocolate Chip Cookie Dough Gooey Bars

My mom has told me multiple times that when she was pregnant with me, she craved chocolate chip cookie dough nightly. She and my dad would sit together on the couch, eating gobs of cookie dough. This was in 1990 when people did outrageous things like eat raw eggs, something I would advise against nowadays so your children don't turn out like me. (KIDDING, I am awesome.) It's literally in my genetic upbringing to love chocolate chip cookie dough, and boy, do I—just like Mom. These bars are for my mom— my best friend, my number one, and the person who introduced me to one of my favorite foods. **15 BARS**

INGREDIENTS

1 box yellow cake mix

½ cup (1 stick) butter, melted

1 egg

FOR FILLING & TOPPING

1 package (24-count) refrigerated chocolate chip cookie dough, room temperature (see Note)

1 (8-ounce) package cream cheese, room temperature

3 eggs

1 teaspoon vanilla extract

½ cup (1 stick) butter, melted

1 (16-ounce) box powdered sugar (plus additional sugar for garnish, if desired)

NOTE: Tired of regular chocolate chip cookie dough? Use peanut butter cookie dough, chocolate cookie dough, or even turtle cookie dough to switch things up!

1. Preheat oven to 350 degrees F. Line a 9×13" baking pan with foil, extending the sides of the foil over the edges of the pan. Spray the foil with cooking spray.

2. In a large bowl, stir together the yellow cake mix, melted butter, and egg with a spatula until combined. Press evenly into the prepared pan to form a crust.

3. Rip off pieces of the chocolate chip cookie dough and press each in the palm of your hand to form a flat piece of dough. Arrange the dough in a single, even layer on top of the crust. Set aside briefly.

4. In the bowl of a stand mixer, beat the cream cheese until fluffy, about 1 minute. Beat in the eggs, one at a time, and then the vanilla extract. Lastly, beat in the butter and powdered sugar until combined. Pour the mixture evenly over the cookie dough and crust layers.

5. Bake for approximately 30 to 35 minutes or until the top is light golden brown. The center will be really jiggly—this is okay! Do *not* over-bake, as this will continue to firm up as it cools.

6. Allow the bars to cool completely, then refrigerate for at least two hours or overnight before cutting into bars. Dust with powdered sugar, if desired, before serving.

Chocolate-Filled Peanut Butter Cookie Bars

I remember the first time I tried Nutella. It was in my sophomore French class, and we were being rewarded with homemade crêpes for some reason. Whenever there's fresh food and a group involved, I become *really* competitive about getting food first. This is the only time I'm competitive, which made me terrible at sports because I just didn't care. While everyone was busy living their lives not surrounded by the prospects of food, I was first in line to get a crêpe with this luscious, mystery filling. One bite and I was hooked—it was so good! Little did I know that this once-unknown spread would become a phenomenon in a few years. Now it's the star in these cookie bars, which you will want to be first in line to get! **9 BARS**

INGREDIENTS

2 (16-ounce) packages refrigerated peanut butter cookie dough, room temperature

1 (13-ounce) jar Nutella or chocolate hazelnut spread of your choosing

NOTE: Some supermarkets sell plain refrigerated peanut butter cookie dough, but most sell the kind with Reese's Pieces or chocolate chips in it. Feel free to use either of those versions!

1. Preheat oven to 350 degrees F. Line an 8×8" or 9×9" baking pan with foil, extending the sides of the foil over the edges of the pan. Spray the foil liberally with cooking spray.

2. Open one package of the cookie dough and press it into a single, even layer at the bottom of the prepared pan. Spoon the Nutella over the cookie dough layer. You may want to spoon the Nutella into a separate bowl and microwave it briefly to soften it.

3. Top the Nutella layer with the second package of cookie dough, pressing into an even layer. Bake for approximately 35 to 40 minutes or until the top is golden and the center is mostly set—it may be a little jiggly still; this is okay as it will continue to set as it cools. Cool completely in the pan before cutting into squares or bars.

Maple Walnut Blondies

Even though I'm a dessert food blogger, I almost never order desserts at restaurants. I know, I know. The way I see it, most restaurants have the same ol' stuff on their menus and I just get bored of it all. Plus, if there's a toss-up between ordering a second Midori Sour or ordering an ice cream sundae, I'm sorry, but Midori wins every time. I freaking love the stuff. The last time I went to a famous chain restaurant, I noticed these blondies on the menu and had to have them. They were soft, chewy, a little gooey, and studded with white chocolate and crunchy walnuts. The whole shebang was topped with ice cream and smothered in this maple sauce that gave me an epiphany: I had to make this at home. You're welcome. 15 BARS

INGREDIENTS

1 cup (2 sticks) butter

2 cups brown sugar

2 eggs

1 teaspoon vanilla extract

2 teaspoons maple extract (see Note)

2 cups all-purpose flour

1 teaspoon baking soda

½ teaspoon salt

½ cup white chocolate chips

½ cup chopped walnuts

FOR MAPLE SAUCE

⅓ cup butter

½ cup sugar

½ cup brown sugar

¼ cup maple syrup

4 ounces cream cheese, cut into cubes

FOR TOPPING

Vanilla ice cream

NOTE: If you're wondering whether or not maple extract is needed in this recipe, it is! Maple extract is highly concentrated maple flavor and there's really no substitute. You can find it in the supermarket next to the vanilla extract.

1. Preheat oven to 350 degrees F. Liberally grease a 9×13" baking pan with cooking spray. Set aside.

2. Melt the butter in a large saucepan over medium heat, stirring to prevent burning. Let cool for about 5 minutes. Stir in the brown sugar, then one egg at a time, and then the vanilla and maple extracts. Lastly, stir in the flour, baking soda, and salt until combined. Fold in the white chocolate chips and walnuts.

3. Spread the batter evenly into the prepared pan and bake for approximately 20 to 25 minutes or until a toothpick inserted near the center comes out clean. Cool in the pan completely.

4. While the blondies cool, make your maple sauce. In a medium saucepan, melt together the butter, sugar, brown sugar, and maple syrup over medium heat, stirring constantly to prevent scorching. Once butter has melted, whisk in the cream cheese and continue whisking until cream cheese melts. Remove from the heat and let sit for about 5 minutes or until thickened.

5. To serve, cut blondies into squares or bars and serve with a scoop of vanilla ice cream and a helping of maple sauce.

Caramel Candy Magic Bars

One Christmas I received a magic set. It was a princess magic set, because we all know that playing magic is a princess's favorite pastime. I practiced all afternoon so I could perform a show later that evening. Long story short, I couldn't get the tricks right. I went out guns blazing, ready to wow my family with a classic coin trick, but I ended up flubbing everything and feeling mortally embarrassed for being a magic fraud. The magic set was never used after that night. One magical thing I don't flub? Magic bars. They're so simple to make, and this Twix version is absolutely incredible. Gooey, chewy, and loaded with chocolate and caramel, it's the real star of the show. **15 BARS**

INGREDIENTS

1 box white cake mix

1 egg

½ cup oil

FOR TOPPING

16 shortbread cookies, coarsely chopped (about 1 cup)

1 cup caramel bits

1 cup semi-sweet chocolate chips

3 Twix bars, roughly chopped (about 1 cup)

1 (14-ounce) can sweetened condensed milk

1. Preheat oven to 350 degrees F. Line a 9 × 13" baking pan with foil, extending the sides of the foil over the edges of the pan. Spray the foil liberally with cooking spray. Set aside.

2. In a large bowl, mix together the cake mix, egg, and oil with a spatula until combined. Press the mixture evenly into the prepared pan and bake for approximately 10 to 12 minutes or until it's lightly golden brown and slightly puffy. Remove from the oven, but keep the oven on.

3. Top the crust with the chopped shortbread cookies, caramel bits, chocolate chips, and Twix bars in an even layer. Drizzle with the sweetened condensed milk.

4. Bake for approximately 18 to 20 minutes or until bubbly and golden. Cool completely in the pan before cutting into bars.

Hot Fudge Slow Cooker Brownies

I love my slow cooker—it's easily one of my favorite appliances. The only thing I dislike about it is actually something I dislike about me—I forget to turn it on half the time. There have been numerous occasions when I've come home after a long day, so excited to eat my slow-cooked meal . . . only to find the darn thing was never turned on. Thankfully, most people can remember to turn on their slow cookers and thus, this recipe is for you guys! The brownie batter comes together in seconds and within a few hours you'll have gooey, molten lava-like brownies to enjoy. SERVES 8

INGREDIENTS

1 box fudge brownie mix

⅔ cup oil

¼ cup water

2 eggs

¾ cup hot water

1 (12-ounce) jar hot fudge sauce

FOR TOPPING

Vanilla ice cream and chocolate sauce, for serving

1. Liberally grease a large slow cooker with cooking spray. In a large bowl, combine the fudge brownie mix, oil, water, and eggs until combined and glossy. Pour the batter into the prepared slow cooker.

2. Meanwhile, whisk together the hot water and the jar of hot fudge sauce until smooth. Pour over the brownie batter. Top with the lid and cook on HIGH for 3 to 3.5 hours or until the edges are set. The center will be gooey—this is okay!

3. Spoon onto a plate or bowl and serve with ice cream and chocolate sauce.

Peanut Butter Snickerdoodle Bars

This recipe goes out to all my pals who love weird food combinations. All the peanut butter and mint jelly sandwich eaters, the chicken nuggets and chocolate shake dunkers, the pickle and cheese cracker stackers, and the hot dogs with a side of mayo peeps. As a kid, one of my favorite combinations was chunky peanut butter on top of cinnamon graham crackers. Okay, it isn't *that* weird, but it is a combination that deserves to be celebrated. Here you have it—chewy, soft peanut butter blondies filled with lots of aromatic cinnamon. **15 BARS**

INGREDIENTS

1 cup (2 sticks) butter

½ cup creamy peanut butter

1 cup brown sugar

2 eggs

1 tablespoon vanilla extract

1 teaspoon baking soda

1 teaspoon ground cinnamon

2 cups all-purpose flour

FOR TOPPING

⅓ cup sugar

1 teaspoon ground cinnamon

NOTE: Want more texture? Feel free to add in chopped nuts, peanut butter chips, or even cinnamon chips!

1. Preheat oven to 350 degrees F. Liberally grease a 9×13" baking pan with cooking spray and set aside.

2. Meanwhile, in a medium saucepan, melt the butter and peanut butter over medium heat until completely melted. Cool for about 5 minutes, then stir in the brown sugar until mixture is combined. Add in the eggs, one at a time, and then the vanilla extract, baking soda, 1 teaspoon ground cinnamon, and the flour, stirring until combined.

3. Spread the batter evenly into the prepared baking pan. In a small bowl, whisk together ⅓ cup sugar and 1 teaspoon cinnamon; sprinkle the mixture evenly and liberally over the blondie batter.

4. Bake for approximately 20 to 22 minutes or until a toothpick inserted near the center comes out clean or with moist—not wet—crumbs. Cool in the pan completely before cutting into squares.

The Easiest Carmelitas Ever

If you can believe it, there was once a time I thought I didn't like caramel, which is probably the most embarrassing of all my confessions. I'm so glad those days are behind me. Growing up, I hadn't heard of carmelitas before—in fact, it wasn't until I became a blogger that I realized these were basically the best concoction ever. Chewy chocolate-studded cookies surrounding a heavenly layer of thick, gooey caramel . . . what could be better? I've shortened the process of making carmelitas from scratch with this totally foolproof, three-ingredient recipe. You'll thank me later. **15 BARS**

INGREDIENTS

1 (30-ounce) package refrigerated chocolate chip cookie dough roll, room temperature

FOR CARAMEL FILLING

1 (11-ounce) package caramel bits

⅓ cup sweetened condensed milk (see Note)

NOTE: Not sure what to do with the remaining sweetened condensed milk? Make Magic Bar Cookies (page 113) or Pink Frosted Lemonade (page 156).

1. Preheat oven to 350 degrees F. Line a 9×13" baking pan with foil, extending the sides of the foil over the edges of the pan. Spray the foil liberally with cooking spray.

2. Cut the cookie dough roll in half, then spread one half of the roll into the prepared pan in an even layer. Bake for approximately 10 minutes, or until golden. Remove from the oven, but keep the oven on.

3. While the cookie layer bakes, make your caramel filling. In a microwave-safe bowl, heat the caramel bits and the sweetened condensed milk together on high heat for 45 seconds. Stir, then heat again for another 30 seconds. Stir until melted and smooth.

4. Pour the caramel mixture over the cookie layer, spreading to cover the pan. Cut the remaining cookie dough roll half into slices and place the slices over the caramel layer, pinching the space between the cookie dough together to form one cohesive piece of cookie dough. It's okay if some of the caramel peeks through, but try your best to fully cover it.

5. Bake for another 15 to 20 minutes or until the top is golden brown and the center isn't wiggly. Cool completely, then refrigerate for at least 2 hours, preferably overnight, before cutting into bars. These definitely need time to cool and set, or else they'll be a gooey (but delicious!) mess.

Mint Chocolate Chip Bars

When it's hot, I always reach for the ice cream, and I'm talking multiple times a day. They say summertime is bikini season, but for me, it's the time of year when I work on my ice cream body. My favorite summertime ice cream flavor? Mint chocolate chip, hands down. There's something so satisfying about that neon green ice cream, and something so refreshing about mint. These bars are named after my favorite summertime staple, and I'm not opposed to nixing the frosting and putting ice cream on top. **15 BARS**

INGREDIENTS

1 box chocolate cake mix

2 eggs

½ cup oil

1 teaspoon mint extract

⅔ cup green mint chips (see Note)

1 cup Andes mint pieces, divided

FOR MINT FROSTING

½ cup (1 stick) butter, room temperature

1 teaspoon vanilla extract

2 teaspoons mint extract

3½–4 cups powdered sugar

¼ cup heavy cream or milk (may not use all of it)

2–3 drops green food coloring

NOTE: The green mint chips are made by the brand Guittard, and are typically found in the baking aisle near all the chocolate chips. If you cannot find them, use dark chocolate mint chips or chocolate chips.

1. Preheat oven to 350 degrees F. Liberally grease a 9×13" baking pan with cooking spray. Set aside.

2. In a large bowl, combine the cake mix, eggs, oil, and mint extract with a spatula until combined. Fold in the green mint chips and ½ cup of Andes mint pieces. Spread the batter into the prepared pan in an even layer.

3. Bake for approximately 15 to 20 minutes or until the top is puffy and set. Cool completely before cutting into bars.

4. Frost or pipe the frosting (recipe below) onto the bars; sprinkle with the remaining ½ cup of Andes mint pieces.

MINT FROSTING

1. In the bowl of a stand mixer, cream together the butter, and vanilla and mint extracts until smooth and creamy, about 2 minutes. Gradually add in the powdered sugar, 1 cup at a time, until frosting is light and fluffy. Add in the cream or milk one tablespoon at a time if frosting is too thick. Lastly, beat in a couple drops of green food coloring, tinting to your desired shade.

Blissful Cranberry Bars

When I was in middle school, some mornings mom would take me to Starbucks. Ah, middle school—nothing like a preteen girl hopped up on caffeine at seven in the morning before she spends her entire day being lanky and awkward. I would always order the blended frappe drinks and the cranberry bars when they were in season. If you've never tried one, you're in for a treat—a chewy, brown sugary blondie base topped with a white chocolate cream cheese and cranberries. Heavenly. 15 BARS

INGREDIENTS

1 cup (2 sticks) butter

1 cup brown sugar

2 eggs

1 tablespoon vanilla extract

1 teaspoon baking soda

Pinch salt

2 cups all-purpose flour

½ cup dried cranberries

½ cup white chocolate chips

FOR WHITE CHOCOLATE CREAM CHEESE FROSTING

½ cup white chocolate chips

6 ounces cream cheese, room temperature

1 teaspoon vanilla extract

3–3½ cups powdered sugar

FOR TOPPING

½ cup dried cranberries

½ cup white chocolate chips

1. Preheat oven to 350 degrees F. Liberally grease a 9×13" baking pan with cooking spray and set aside.

2. In a large saucepan, melt the butter over medium heat. Cool for about 5 minutes. Stir in the brown sugar to combine, then the eggs, one at a time. Stir in the vanilla, baking soda, salt, and flour until combined. Fold in the dried cranberries and white chocolate chips.

3. Spread the batter evenly in the prepared pan and bake for approximately 20 to 22 minutes or until a toothpick inserted near the center comes out clean or with moist—not wet—crumbs. Cool completely.

4. Once bars are cool, make your frosting according to recipe below. Spread the frosting over the bars in an even layer; top with the remaining cranberries. In a small bowl, melt ½ cup white chocolate chips. Pour the melted white chocolate chips into a plastic sandwich bag, seal out the air, snip off the tip, and drizzle the melted white chocolate over the bars. Place in the fridge for about 1 hour to set, then cut into wedges or bars and serve. Store covered in the refrigerator.

WHITE CHOCOLATE CREAM CHEESE FROSTING

1. In a large microwave-safe bowl, melt ½ cup of white chocolate chips in 30-second increments, stirring after each increment, until melted. Add in the cream cheese, vanilla, and 1 cup of the powdered sugar and beat with an electric mixer until combined. Gradually add in the remaining powdered sugar until a soft and fluffy frosting is achieved.

Dulce de Leche Brownies

I was a grown adult by the time I had dulce de leche, and that's just criminal . . . kind of like wearing socks with sandals, or talking on the phone while ordering something in a restaurant. Now that I've had a taste of that sweet, caramelized nectar, I can't stop eating it. I buy a jar for a recipe and by the time I'm ready to bake said recipe, I've already eaten half of the jar. True story. If you can manage to save your dulce de leche for this recipe, I highly suggest you do—these brownies are outstanding! Super fudgy, chewy, and packed with caramel candies and a dulce de leche swirl. Don't hold off on trying dulce de leche like I did! **9 BARS**

INGREDIENTS

1 box chocolate cake mix

1 egg

½ cup (1 stick) butter, melted

FOR TOPPING

30 Rolos, unwrapped and cut in half

1 (7–8-ounce) can prepared dulce de leche, divided

1 (14-ounce) can sweetened condensed milk

NOTE: Because these brownies are super fudgy and gooey, you may want to wait for the brownies to set up overnight before cutting into bars.

1. Preheat oven to 350 degrees F. Line an 8×8" or 9×9" baking pan with foil, extending the sides of the foil over the edges of the pan. Spray the foil liberally with cooking spray. Set aside.

2. In a large bowl, combine the cake mix, egg, and melted butter with a spatula until a soft dough forms. Press ¾ of the dough into the prepared pan in an even layer; top with the halved Rolo candies.

3. In a medium bowl, whisk together half of the can of dulce de leche and the full can of sweetened condensed milk until smooth. Pour the mixture evenly over the Rolo candies. Crumble the remaining dough on top, trying to cover the condensed milk layer as completely as possible. It's okay if some of the condensed milk mixture peeks through.

4. Bake for approximately 30 to 35 minutes or until the center appears mostly set—if it jiggles a little bit, that's okay. Cool completely in the pan before cutting into bars (see Note). Once cut, drizzle with remaining dulce de leche.

Toffee Shortbread Bars

I used to work in a frozen yogurt shop, and for the most part, the job was pretty awesome. For starters, I was able to get a free froyo every day I worked. Although my coworkers warned me that I'd grow tired of it, I made myself a froyo creation every day for two years. There weren't many flavors I didn't like; in fact, I was non-discriminatory when it came to soft serve. One flavor that we rarely had but was always a treat was butter brickle. It's a sweet toffee flavor that paired beautifully with caramel sauce and toffee bits, and whenever I could sneak in a sample cup of the stuff, I would—which was all the time. Make these shortbread bars—they have the same warm toffee flavor and they'd taste great crumbled over ice cream! **24 BARS**

INGREDIENTS

2 cups (4 sticks) butter, room temperature

1 cup powdered sugar

1 teaspoon butter extract

1 teaspoon vanilla extract

½ cup cornstarch

3½ cups all-purpose flour

1 cup toffee bits

1. Preheat oven to 325 degrees F. Lightly grease a 15 × 10" rimmed baking pan with cooking spray. Set aside.

2. In the bowl of a stand mixer, cream together the butter and powdered sugar until soft and smooth. Add in the butter and vanilla extracts and beat to combine. Lastly, add in the cornstarch and flour, 1 cup at a time, until dough is soft and combined. Stir in the toffee bits.

3. Press the mixture evenly onto the prepared pan; prick holes all over the dough with a fork.

4. Bake for approximately 35 to 40 minutes or until shortbread bars are golden brown. Cool completely before cutting into bar shapes or wedges.

Classic Seven Layer Bars

I still remember the first time I made a seven layer bar. It was a chocolate peanut butter version and after one bite, I was hooked on the stuff. They are surprisingly addictive, like getting tattoos and adopting puppies. It wasn't long before I was trying to come up with as many different flavor combinations as humanly possible. Here is my take on the original version, which consists of butterscotch chips, chocolate chips, coconut, pecans, graham crackers, a buttery base, and sweetened condensed milk drizzled all up on that business. Also known as "magic bars" or "Hello Dolly" bars, I affectionately refer to them as "get in my mouth-hole bars." **15 BARS**

INGREDIENTS

1 box yellow cake mix

1 egg

½ cup oil

FOR TOPPING

½ cup graham cracker crumbs

1 cup shredded coconut

⅔ cup semi-sweet chocolate chips

⅔ cup butterscotch chips

⅔ cup chopped pecans

1 (14-ounce) can sweetened
  condensed milk

NOTE: Want more flavor ideas? Use chocolate cake mix and top with chopped mint candies and mint chips! You can also try a chocolate peanut butter version with peanut butter cups, peanut butter chips, and a couple tablespoons of creamy peanut butter mixed in with the sweetened condensed milk.

1. Preheat oven to 350 degrees F. Line a 9×13" baking pan with foil, extending the sides of the foil over the edges of the pan. Spray the foil liberally with cooking spray. Set aside.

2. In a large bowl, combine the cake mix, egg, and oil with a spatula until combined. Press the dough into the prepared pan in an even layer and bake for approximately 10 to 12 minutes. Remove from the oven, but keep the oven on.

3. First, sprinkle the graham cracker crumbs and shredded coconut evenly over the base. Then evenly sprinkle the chocolate chips, butterscotch chips, and pecans. Drizzle with the sweetened condensed milk.

4. Return to the oven and bake for approximately 18 to 20 minutes, or until the top is bubbly and set. Cool completely in the pan before cutting into squares.

Cookie Truffle Brownies

I remember when cake pops came out—they were all the rage and everyone everywhere was making them, myself included. The concept is pretty genius: bake a cake or crush some cookies, mix in cream cheese, and voila— you have cake pops. Then there's the whole execution part—that's where it gets dicey. Rolling, dipping, adding sticks . . . These have that truffle-y, cake pop-y goodness without all the hassle. If you're a chocoholic, you'll flip over these insanely chocolaty brownies. **9–12 BARS**

INGREDIENTS

1 box chocolate fudge brownie mix, plus ingredients listed in package directions

¼ cup hot fudge sundae sauce

FOR FILLING

20 Oreo cookies

4 ounces cream cheese, room temperature

FOR TOPPING

½ cup semi-sweet chocolate chips

3 tablespoons heavy cream

½ cup miniature chocolate chips

NOTE: These are easily adaptable to whichever flavor of Oreo is your favorite! Try mint Oreos, peanut butter Oreos, golden Oreos, or even birthday cake Oreos for a special twist!

1. Preheat oven to 350 degrees F. Liberally grease an 8×8" or 9×9" baking pan with cooking spray. Set aside.

2. In a large bowl, prepare the brownie mix according to package directions. Stir the hot fudge sundae sauce into the brownie batter to combine. Pour the batter into the prepared pan and bake for approximately 30 to 40 minutes or until a toothpick inserted near the center comes out clean or with moist—not wet—crumbs. Cool completely.

3. After brownies have cooled, make your cookie truffle filling. In a food processor, pulse the Oreo cookies until ground crumbs appear. Add in the softened cream cheese and pulse until moistened and combined.

4. Spread the filling on top of the brownies evenly. Set aside.

5. Meanwhile, make your topping: In a medium, microwave-safe bowl, melt the semi-sweet chocolate chips and the heavy cream in the microwave for 45 seconds, stirring well until melted and smooth. Pour the ganache over the truffle layer, spreading it to the edges. Sprinkle immediately with the miniature chocolate chips.

6. Place in the refrigerator for about 2 hours to set before cutting into squares.

Gooey Chocolate Chip Pecan Pie Bars

I love making these for the holidays. In my house, we usually enjoy apple and pumpkin pies, but last year I switched things up and made Pecan Pie Bars. You gotta keep your loved ones on their toes, right? Turns out, everyone loved the change and really, what's not to love? The bars are supremely gooey and rich, studded with lots of crunchy pecans and chocolate chips. I finished them off with a drizzle of salted caramel sauce because you only live once. **15 BARS**

INGREDIENTS

1 (30-ounce) roll refrigerated chocolate chip cookie dough, room temperature

FOR FILLING

1 cup brown sugar

1 cup dark corn syrup

½ cup (1 stick) butter, melted

4 eggs

1 teaspoon vanilla extract

2 cups chopped pecans

1 cup semi-sweet chocolate chips

FOR TOPPING

½ (12-ounce) jar salted caramel sauce (see Note)

NOTE: If you can't find salted caramel sauce, use regular caramel sauce and sprinkle with sea salt before serving.

1. Preheat oven to 350 degrees F. Line a 9 × 13" baking pan with foil, extending the sides of the foil over the edges of the pan. Spray the foil liberally with cooking spray.

2. To prepare the crust, press the cookie dough roll evenly into the prepared pan and bake for approximately 10 to 15 minutes or until golden and puffy. Remove from the oven but keep the oven on.

3. While crust bakes, make your filling. In a large bowl, whisk together the brown sugar, corn syrup, melted butter, eggs, and vanilla until blended. Fold in the chopped pecans and chocolate chips.

4. Pour the filling mixture evenly over the crust layer and carefully return to the oven. Bake for approximately 25 to 30 minutes or until the top is golden and appears set. It may be slightly wiggly, but that's okay—do not over-bake. Cool completely, then refrigerate for at least two hours or until set.

5. Just before serving, drizzle with salted caramel sauce.

Gooey Lemon Bars

Lemon desserts are one of my favorite types of desserts. There's something so refreshing and satisfying about a sweet-tart lemon treat any time of the year. But what I don't like? Savory lemon dishes. Lemon has no place on my chicken or in my pasta. I'm a lemon-in-a-sweet-tea and lemon-in-my-cake kinda girl through and through—so y'all can take your lemon pepper and ride off into the sunset happily ever after. Meanwhile, I'm going to be content with these Lemon Bars. They're rich, ultra gooey, and bursting with fresh lemon flavor. They're the perfect treat for the Fourth of July, too. **15 BARS**

INGREDIENTS

1 box lemon cake mix

1 egg

½ cup (1 stick) butter, melted

FOR FILLING

1 (8-ounce) package cream cheese, room temperature

3 eggs

1 (16-ounce) box powdered sugar, plus more for dusting

¼ cup butter, melted

¼ cup lemon juice

Zest of 1 lemon

1. Preheat oven to 350 degrees F. Line a 9 × 13" baking pan with foil, extending the foil over the edges of the pan. Spray the foil liberally with cooking spray.

2. In a large bowl, combine the cake mix, egg, and melted butter until a soft dough forms. Spread the mixture evenly into the prepared pan. Set aside.

3. Meanwhile, in another large bowl, beat the cream cheese, eggs, and powdered sugar together on LOW speed for about 1 minute, or until combined. Stream in the melted butter, lemon juice, and lemon zest and beat to combine, until thick. Pour the mixture on top of the crust layer.

4. Bake for approximately 35 to 40 minutes or until the top is light golden brown and the center is just about set. It will be a little wiggly—that's okay. You do not want to overbake these as they're called gooey bars for a reason.

5. Cool the bars completely, then refrigerate for at least 2 hours or until set. Just before serving, dust with additional powdered sugar.

Salted Caramel Crispy Treats

Oh, high school—you couldn't pay me enough money to go back and experience all of that again, especially teenage heartbreak. I remember when my sophomore boyfriend broke up with me during my freshmen year and I thought my world was over—never mind that we only dated for about two months. (Note that drama has always been a subject I excelled in.) To mend my broken heart, I would sometimes steal the caramel sauce out of the fridge and eat it with a spoon, as if excess amounts of caramel would cure my hurt feelings. Let's face it, it certainly helped. If caramel can help heal a broken heart, it's practically a health food. These Salted Caramel Crispy Treats are made with that luscious salted caramel, so there's no shortage of the glorious golden stuff here. Even if you're not pining, make them—you'll be glad you did! **15 BARS**

INGREDIENTS

¼ cup (½ stick) butter

1 (10-ounce) bag miniature marshmallows, plus 1 cup, divided

1 (12-ounce) jar salted caramel sauce, divided (see Note)

6 cups Rice Krispies cereal

NOTE: If you can't find salted caramel sauce, use regular caramel sauce and sprinkle with sea salt before serving.

1. Lightly grease a 9×13" baking pan with cooking spray and set aside. In a large saucepan, melt the butter and bag of marshmallows together over medium heat, stirring occasionally, until smooth. Stir in ½ cup of the salted caramel sauce to combine.

2. While marshmallow mixture melts, add the cereal to a large bowl. Pour the melted marshmallow mixture into the cereal bowl. Add in the remaining cup of marshmallows and stir to combine. Mixture will be very sticky.

3. Press the mixture into the prepared pan—I like to use the bottom of a greased glass to press it in—and let set at room temperature for about 1 hour. Drizzle with remaining salted caramel before cutting into squares.

Mocha Brownie Tiramisu

For the longest time, I naïvely thought I wouldn't like tiramisu. I also naïvely thought that I'd marry Justin Timberlake or have my own fashion line (never mind that I don't even know how to sew on a button). Neither of the former happened, but I can now proudly say that I love tiramisu—it's one of my favorite desserts. On my blog, I've made Twinkie Tiramisu, Donut Tiramisu, even Oatmeal Crème Pie Tiramisu—so a brownie version was bound to happen. Fudgy brownies soak up all that wonderful coffee and chocolate flavor and are the perfect substitute for ladyfingers. SERVES 9

INGREDIENTS

1 (9×13") pan fudge brownies, baked and cooled

½ cup hot fudge sundae sauce, divided

½ cup strongly brewed coffee, room temperature, divided

FOR FILLING

1 (12-ounce) package whipped cream cheese, room temperature

½ cup sugar

1 tablespoon vanilla extract

1 teaspoon ground cinnamon

1 (8-ounce) package Cool Whip, thawed

FOR TOPPING

Cocoa powder and hot fudge

NOTE: For an after-hours version, add ¼ cup Kahlua or other coffee liqueur.

1. Line an 8×8" pan with foil, extending the sides of the foil over the edges of the pan. Mist the foil lightly with cooking spray. Cut the pan of baked brownies into 15 equal pieces, trimming away the tougher edges. Take a piece of brownie and flatten it in your palm; place it into the foil-lined pan. Repeat with 6 more brownies, forming a single layer on the bottom of the foil-lined pan. Use half of one brownie to complete the layer, if needed.

2. Drizzle half of the hot fudge sauce and half of the coffee evenly over the brownies. In a medium bowl, beat together the cream cheese, sugar, vanilla extract, and cinnamon until blended, about 1 minute. Fold in Cool Whip. Spread half of this mixture on top of the brownie layer.

3. Repeat the brownie layer once more, using the remaining half brownie if needed. Drizzle with the remaining fudge and coffee, then top with the cream cheese mixture. Dust with cocoa powder and refrigerate for at least 6 hours or until set. Just before serving, drizzle with hot fudge, if desired.

Cookie Tips & Tricks

In this chapter, you'll find a mixture of recipes that are homemade and that start with a cookie mix. In most homemade recipes, you can use a cookie mix instead, if desired. Just simply follow the directions on the back of the package and stir in the add-ins from the recipe. Bake as directed on the package.

* Cornstarch is my secret ingredient in the homemade cookies. It creates a thick, fluffy cookie and is necessary in my recipes.

* When it comes to homemade cookie dough, chilling the dough is mandatory for at LEAST 2 hours, up to overnight. Chilling prevents the dough from spreading too thin in the oven, resulting in a flat, crispy cookie.

* I like baking my cookies on light metal baking sheets with silicone liners on top. This creates an evenly baked cookie with a light golden brown bottom. If you don't have silicone liners, feel free to use parchment paper or lightly grease the cookie sheets with cooking spray.

* The cooking time in my cookie recipes produces chewy, soft cookies. If you prefer yours a little on the crisper side, leave them in for 1 to 3 minutes longer, depending on how crisp you want them.

* *Always* rotate your cookie sheets halfway during the baking time to ensure an evenly baked cookie.

* For the most consistent product, I recommend using a one- or two-tablespoon-size cookie dough scoop. They're less than $10 and are one of my most-used kitchen tools.

3

Chewy, Crispy, and Everything Good Cookies

Peanut Butter Cup-Stuffed Chocolate Chip Cookies

Once upon a time, when I was in high school and still thought teasing my hair was trendy, I liked the gym. I would run for miles and miles on the treadmill like there was a donut dangling at the end of the finish line. I would do squats for fun. I was a demon on the elliptical. Now you couldn't bribe me with a chocolate layer cake to even step a *foot* in gym sneakers. So what do I do with my spare time? Make cookies, of course! Making (and eating) these Peanut Butter Cup-Stuffed Chocolate Chip Cookies are just the perfect way to spend my new time. **12–14 COOKIES**

INGREDIENTS

1 cup (2 sticks) butter, room temperature

1 cup brown sugar

½ cup sugar

1 egg

1 tablespoon vanilla extract

1 teaspoon baking soda

2 teaspoons cornstarch

½ teaspoon salt

2¼ cups all-purpose flour

1 cup semi-sweet chocolate chips

12–14 snack-size peanut butter cups, unwrapped

FOR TOPPING

1 square chocolate candy coating/ almond bark

1 square vanilla candy coating/almond bark

1 tablespoon creamy peanut butter

1. In the bowl of a stand mixer, cream together the butter and sugars until creamy and smooth, about 2 minutes. Beat in the egg and vanilla until combined. Lastly, beat in the baking soda, cornstarch, salt, and flour to combine. Fold in the chocolate chips.

2. Refrigerate the cookie dough for at least 2 hours, up to overnight. This is mandatory.

3. Preheat oven to 350 degrees F. Line 2 baking sheets with parchment paper or silicone liners. Using a cookie dough scoop, portion out a tablespoon of cookie dough and flatten it in the palm of your hand. Place a peanut butter cup on top, then top the peanut butter cup with another flattened tablespoon of dough, enclosing the peanut butter cup inside. Place the dough balls onto the baking sheets about 2" apart.

4. Bake for approximately 10 to 12 minutes, rotating pans halfway through baking time, until golden brown. Cookies will appear soft and a little gooey; this is normal and they'll continue to set up as they cool. Cool completely.

5. Just before serving, melt the chocolate bark and vanilla bark in separate bowls. Stir the peanut butter into the vanilla bark. Drizzle the chocolate and vanilla mixture evenly over the cookies.

Cake Batter Gooey Butter Cookies

I'm a cake batter fiend and have been since I was a little girl. When my mom made a cake (which was a special occasion in itself), she'd always let me lick the beaters. It was such a treat to be able to savor that sweet, battery nectar just before eating the finished, fluffy cake. To this day, I still lick the beaters after I make a cake or cookies. It's like the universe is rewarding you for baking, saying "Here, have a little pregame snack before you shovel all those cookies in your face while binge-watching your DVR." To go against the universe is kind of scary, so I happily oblige. These cookies taste just like cake batter, thanks to their gooey texture. I use the classic Funfetti cake mix, but you can use any flavor you'd like! **20–24 COOKIES**

INGREDIENTS

1 box Funfetti cake mix (see Note)

1 (8-ounce) package cream cheese, room temperature

½ cup butter, softened

1 teaspoon vanilla extract

1 teaspoon butter extract

1 egg

1 cup powdered sugar

NOTE: Modeled after the famous gooey butter cake from St. Louis, these cookies are traditionally made with yellow cake mix. Feel free to stick to the original or try my Funfetti version, because everyone loves sprinkles.

1. Preheat oven to 350 degrees F. Line 2 baking sheets with parchment paper or silicone liners. Set aside.

2. In a large bowl, combine cake mix, cream cheese, butter, vanilla extract, butter extract, and egg together with an electric mixer until a soft dough forms, about 1 minute.

3. Scoop rounded tablespoons of dough out using a cookie dough scoop. Roll the cookie dough ball into the powdered sugar and place on the baking sheets about 2" apart.

4. Bake for approximately 10 to 12 minutes, rotating pans halfway through baking time. Cool completely before serving.

Galactic Crunch Cookies

I am completely and utterly a child of convenience. Growing up, my family didn't cook often, so we'd frequently visit the drive-thru for our meals. While some people squirm when I tell them that, I don't think it was a bad thing—in fact, it propelled me to learn how to cook for my family. Plus, did your mom's homemade lasagna come with a free toy in a cardboard box? I didn't think so. Clearly, I'm the winner here. Winning aside, one of my favorite after-lunch desserts (don't judge) were Star Crunch Cookies. I'd sneak into my Grammie Pat's cupboard and grab a couple to feast on while watching *Scooby Doo*. I knew I had to recreate this classic cookie as an ode to my childhood. **10–12 COOKIES**

INGREDIENTS

1 (11.5-ounce) bag Milky Way Simply Caramel candy bars, unwrapped and roughly chopped

¼ cup (½ stick) butter

1 (10-ounce) bag miniature marshmallows

6 cups Rice Krispies cereal

FOR TOPPING

2 (16-ounce) packages chocolate candy coating/almond bark

1. Line a baking sheet with parchment paper or a silicone liner. Set aside.

2. In a large bowl, melt the chopped Milky Way caramel candies on HIGH power in the microwave for 30 seconds. Stir, then melt for another 30 seconds. Keep heating in 20- to 30-second increments, stirring after each, until just about melted.

3. Add the butter and marshmallows to the candy mixture and heat again for 30 seconds. Stir, then heat for another 30 seconds or until marshmallows are puffy and melted. Stir until smooth and combined with the candy. Mixture will be thick and caramel colored.

4. Add in the cereal and toss to combine. Working quickly, grab fistfuls (about ½- to ¾-cup size) of the mixture and form each into compact, hamburger-size patties. Place them on the prepared baking sheet and repeat with remaining patties. Let the patties cool and set for about 1 hour.

5. Once set, melt the chocolate bark according to package directions, stirring until melted. Dip the patties into the melted chocolate and, using a fork, coat the patties completely. Use the same fork to gently lift the patties from the chocolate and place them back onto the baking sheet. Repeat with remaining patties.

6. If you have leftover chocolate, drizzle it over the cookies. Let the chocolate set, then serve!

Death by Chocolate Cookies

Serious chocoholics will *flip* for these Death by Chocolate Cookies! I'm not typically a chocoholic, but occasionally (okay, fine—once or twice a week) I'll get a really big hankering for something super rich and chocolaty. Usually I'll fill this craving with underbaked brownies or a slice of chocolate cake, but sometimes I'll whip up these cookies to nosh on because they're so dang rich! That is, if I don't finish off the cookie dough in the meantime. This recipe boasts three different types of chocolate chips for that ultimate chocolate flavor. If you don't think you're a chocoholic, make these cookies and prepare to be converted. **14–16 COOKIES**

INGREDIENTS

1 cup (2 sticks) butter, room temperature

¾ cup brown sugar

¾ cup sugar

2 eggs

1 tablespoon vanilla extract

1 teaspoon baking soda

½ teaspoon salt

1½ cups all-purpose flour

1½ cups dark chocolate cake mix (just the dry mix)

½ cup white chocolate chips

½ cup dark chocolate chips

½ cup semi-sweet chocolate chips

1. In the bowl of a stand mixer, cream together the butter and sugars until smooth and creamy, about 2 minutes. Gradually beat in the eggs, one at a time, and then the vanilla. Lastly, add in the baking soda, salt, flour, and cake mix powder, beating until a soft dough forms. Fold in all of the chips.

2. Refrigerate the cookie dough for at least 2 hours, up to overnight. This is mandatory.

3. Preheat oven to 350 degrees F. Line 2 baking sheets with parchment paper or silicone liners. Drop rounded tablespoons of cookie dough onto the baking sheets about 2" apart. Bake for approximately 10 to 12 minutes, rotating pans halfway through baking time. Cookies will appear soft and a little gooey; this is normal. They'll continue to set up as they cool. Cool completely.

Cherry Pie Cookies

One of my favorite things to do is create two desserts in one. For instance, my Magic Bar Cookies (page 113) which combine the classic magic bar with a soft and chewy cookie. My Mocha Brownie Tiramisu (page 87) which takes fudgy brownies and uses it as the base for tiramisu. Consider me a dessert Dr. Jekyll and Mr. Hyde—I'm sweet and unsuspecting on the outside, but inside, I'm an evil master trying to make the most sinful desserts imaginable. These Cherry Pie Cookies are a result of my Mr. Hyde—two desserts morphed together and masquerading as one. While I prefer the tartness of the juicy cherries, feel free to use any flavor of pie filling you'd like. Apple would taste phenomenal with peanut butter cookie dough! **24 COOKIES**

INGREDIENTS

1 (24-count) package refrigerated sugar cookie dough, room temperature

1 (21-ounce) can cherry pie filling (see Note)

FOR GLAZE (OPTIONAL, BUT RECOMMENDED)

1 cup powdered sugar

1 teaspoon almond extract

2 tablespoons heavy cream

NOTE: Extra pie filling has many great uses! Top brownies or ice cream with it, blend it into a milkshake, garnish Molten Lava Cakes (page 40) with it, or make Black Forest Brownie Cheesecake Bars (page 136) with it!

1. Preheat oven to 350 degrees F. Liberally grease a 24-cavity miniature muffin pan with cooking spray.

2. Place one cookie dough ball into each muffin cavity. Use your fingers to press it down and slightly up the sides in a flat disc. Bake for approximately 10 to 15 minutes or until the edges are golden brown and the center appears set. Once removed from the oven, use the handle of a wooden spoon to make an indentation in the center of each cookie cup. Let cool in the pan for about 15 minutes, then gently ease the cookie cups out with a butter knife. Cool completely on a wire rack.

3. Fill each cookie cup with a generous tablespoon of pie filling. You will have some pie filling leftover—see Note for ideas of uses.

4. Prepare glaze: In a small bowl, whisk together the powdered sugar, almond extract, and heavy cream until a smooth glaze forms; add more cream if needed. Drizzle evenly over the cookie cups and let set, about 15 minutes.

Joyful Almond Macaroons

Let's have a little vocabulary and grammar lesson, shall we? *Definitely* means something is definite; *defiantly* means something is done angrily or out of spite. *Your* is possessive; *you're* describes you. *Macaron* is a French cookie made of almond flour and is sold for the price of a right lung in some bakeries. *Macaroon* is a coconut cookie that's gooey, soft, and chewy, and not at all as pretentious as its one o-less cookie counterpart. While I love macarons, macaroons are also a favorite. They're truly meant for coconut lovers since they're unadulterated coconut baked with sweetened condensed milk for a tender, chewy cookie. These cookies will be YOUR new favorite since YOU'RE someone with good taste—a fact that is DEFINITELY true. **16 COOKIES**

INGREDIENTS

5½ cups shredded coconut

⅔ cup all-purpose flour

1 teaspoon vanilla extract

1 teaspoon almond extract

1 (14-ounce) can sweetened
   condensed milk

FOR TOPPING

16 raw almonds

4 squares chocolate candy coating/
   almond bark

1. Preheat oven to 350 degrees F. Line 2 baking sheets with parchment paper or silicone liners.

2. In a large bowl, toss together the coconut and flour until coated. Stir in the vanilla extract, almond extract, and sweetened condensed milk until combined and sticky, about 1 minute.

3. Drop rounded tablespoons of the coconut mixture onto the baking sheets about 1" apart. Use wet fingers to smooth out the tops of the coconut mounds, which will prevent the ends of the coconut shreds from burning. Place an almond on top of each cookie mound.

4. Bake for approximately 12 to 15 minutes, rotating pans halfway through baking time, until golden brown and fragrant. Cool completely on the sheets.

5. Melt the chocolate bark according to package directions, or until smooth. Dip the bottoms of the cookies into the melted chocolate, then place back on the cookie sheet. Once all the cookies have been dipped, pour the remaining chocolate bark into a plastic sandwich bag, seal out the air, and snip off the tip. Drizzle the remaining chocolate onto the cookies.

Toffee Chip Espresso Cookies

For the longest time, I swore I'd never be a coffee drinker. When I was in college, I somehow managed to wake up at 4:30 a.m., walk my dog, eat breakfast, get ready, and be at school for class by 6:45 a.m. . . . all without coffee. Looking back, I'm surprised I didn't have a superhero cape and a bounty on my head from an evil villain, because I was basically Superwoman. Then one day I had a cup, which transitioned slowly into a cup several times a week to eventually, a cup a day. While I don't exceed 8 ounces of coffee a day, I do need it to function or else I *am* that evil villain. You can imagine my delight knowing I get a lovely caffeinated jolt from these Toffee Chip Espresso Cookies. They're so soft, chewy, and loaded with amazing coffee and toffee flavors. A must-make! **18–20 COOKIES**

INGREDIENTS

1 cup (2 sticks) butter, room temperature

1 cup brown sugar

½ cup sugar

1 egg

1 tablespoon vanilla extract

1 teaspoon baking soda

2 teaspoons cornstarch

½ teaspoon salt

1 tablespoon instant espresso powder (see Note)

2¼ cups all-purpose flour

Heaping ¾ cup chocolate chunks

⅔ cup toffee bits

NOTE: Use as much or as little espresso powder as you like!

1. In the bowl of a stand mixer, cream together the butter and sugars until creamy and smooth, about 2 minutes. Beat in the egg and vanilla until combined. Lastly, beat in the baking soda, cornstarch, salt, espresso powder, and flour to combine. Fold in the chocolate chunks and toffee bits.

2. Refrigerate the cookie dough for at least 2 hours, up to overnight. This is mandatory.

3. Preheat oven to 350 degrees F. Line 2 baking sheets with parchment paper or silicone liners. Using a cookie dough scoop, drop heaping tablespoons of dough about 2" apart on the baking sheets.

4. Bake for approximately 10 to 12 minutes, rotating pans halfway through baking time, until golden brown. Cookies will appear soft and a little gooey; this is normal and they'll continue to set up as they cool. Cool completely.

Red Velvet Crinkle Cookies

I am a sucker for any kind of catchy tune. It doesn't even have to be in my preferred genre of music—if it has a good beat, I'm all about it. This usually means I'll end up liking a song by an artist I don't typically care for, and the denial about liking the song comes soon after. The song will play on the radio and I'll insist the station be changed, but really, I'm hoping it stays on. I just can't admit defeat even though my body is dying to dance to the catchy beat. Likewise, I also latch on to food trends. I was all about the bacon trend, all about the macaron trend, and all about the red velvet trend a few years back. Thankfully, red velvet is a classic that never goes out of style (unlike some of those one-hit wonders) and everyone can learn to love these cookies! **20–24 COOKIES**

INGREDIENTS

1 box red velvet cake mix

2 eggs

½ cup butter, melted

1 cup white chocolate chips

2 cups powdered sugar

1. Preheat oven to 350 degrees F. Line 2 baking sheets with parchment paper or silicone liners.

2. In a large bowl, combine the cake mix, eggs, and melted butter with a spatula until a soft dough forms. Fold in the white chocolate chips.

3. Drop rounded tablespoons of dough into a bowl with the powdered sugar. Coat the dough balls completely in powdered sugar—you shouldn't even see red anymore. Place the coated dough ball onto the baking sheet, about 2" apart.

4. Bake for approximately 8 to 10 minutes, rotating pans halfway through baking time, until cookies appear soft but set. Cool on the pan completely.

Chocolate Mint Cookies

I love the Girl Scouts, even though I wasn't a fan of actually *being* one. Sure, I loved collecting my patches and eating the cookies. (Hello, a girl's gotta endorse her product!) Truth be told, I'm kind of a loner. I like solitude. Quiet. It helps balance the fact that I'm the loudest human being on the planet. Not to mention, there was a lot of competitive team-building. I'm the least competitive person on the planet, which is why I quit my sales job and never played team sports. If there's one thing I still love about Girl Scouts, it's their cookies! My favorites are the Samoas and, of course, Thin Mints. This homemade recipe is SO simple, and it comes together in minutes!

40 COOKIES

INGREDIENTS

20 Oreo cookies

1 (16-ounce) package chocolate candy coating/almond bark

1 teaspoon mint extract

NOTE: What about that extra filling? Well, besides eating it plain, I recommend using it in my Crème-Filled Chocolate Chip Cookies (page 114)!

1. Line a large baking sheet with foil. Carefully twist open the Oreo cookies and scrape the filling into a small bowl. See Note below for a recipe featuring the crème-filling! Place the plain Oreo cookies onto the baking sheet in an even layer.

2. Melt the chocolate bark according to package directions, or until smooth. Quickly stir in the mint extract to combine.

3. Working quickly, dip an Oreo cookie into the chocolate with a fork, covering the cookie completely with the chocolate. Use the fork to lift the Oreo out of the chocolate, allowing excess to drip off. Return the cookie to the baking sheet. Repeat with remaining cookies.

4. Allow chocolate to set, about 10 minutes.

Cappuccino Meringue Cookies

I never understood how people could get work done in a coffee shop. I've tried, and I type maybe two words before I'm distracted by people watching. I applaud those who don't find petty teenage coffee shop drama fascinating, but I can't help myself. This is also probably why I still read young-adult novels and watch preteen dramas on TV. I try my hardest to be sophisticated, but let's face it, I still eat boxed mac & cheese for dinner once a week. I'm no cosmopolitan woman. I envision that posh people eat meringue cookies. They're pillowy soft, slightly chewy, and they melt in your mouth. These taste like one of the most sophisticated coffee drinks there is. Luckily, these cookies don't judge us based on our TV show choices . . . only that we have great taste in cookies. **45 COOKIES**

INGREDIENTS

3 egg whites

¾ cup sugar

¼ teaspoon cream of tartar

1 tablespoon instant espresso powder

FOR TOPPING

About ⅓ cup whole coffee beans

NOTE: Want to make these Mocha Meringues? Simply dip the bottoms in melted chocolate.

1. Preheat oven to 175 degrees F. Line two baking sheets with parchment paper. Set aside.

2. In a large heat-proof bowl sitting over a pot of simmering water, whisk together the egg whites and sugar until frothy, about 30 seconds to 1 minute. Immediately remove from the heat and pour the mixture into the bowl of a stand mixer. Add in the cream of tartar and the espresso powder.

3. Beat the mixture on HIGH speed for 5 to 7 minutes or until meringue has stiff peaks. Spoon the meringue into a piping bag attached with a large open-star tip. Pipe the meringues about the size of a silver dollar onto the baking sheets. Since they don't spread while baking, you can pipe them fairly close together. Top each meringue with a coffee bean.

4. Bake for approximately 50 minutes, then rotate the pans and bake for another 50 minutes or until meringues are dry to the touch and set. Turn off the oven but leave the oven door cracked and allow them to cool completely before serving.

Salted Butterscotch Cookies

Butterscotch reminds me of my Grammie Pat, who made oatmeal scotchie cookies. We only lived two doors down from her, so whenever she'd make a batch, she'd send over a plate. There's something so irresistible about that creamy, caramel-y butterscotch. In fact, one of the first things I ever baked were butterscotch blondies with salt sprinkled on top. HEAVEN. These cookies are both an homage to my Grammie Pat and an ode to my early baking days. While they don't have oatmeal, I wouldn't be opposed to adding some in. **18 COOKIES**

INGREDIENTS

1 (14–17.5-ounce) package sugar cookie mix (see Note)

½ cup (1 stick) butter, room temperature

1 egg

2 tablespoons heavy cream or milk

1 (3.4-ounce) box instant butterscotch pudding mix

¾ cup butterscotch chips

FOR TOPPING

Sea salt, for sprinkling

NOTE: If you're craving oatmeal scotchies, make these with oatmeal cookie mix!

1. Preheat oven to 350 degrees F. Line 2 baking sheets with parchment paper or silicone liners. Set aside.

2. In a large bowl, mix together the sugar cookie mix, butter, egg, heavy cream, and dry butterscotch pudding mix until a soft dough forms. Fold in the butterscotch chips.

3. Drop heaping tablespoons of cookie dough onto the baking sheets, about 2" apart. Sprinkle the tops of the dough balls with a healthy pinch of sea salt.

4. Bake for approximately 10 to 12 minutes, rotating pans halfway through baking time, or until cookies appear set. Cookies may look soft, but that's okay—you don't want to over-bake these. Cool completely on the baking sheet.

Magic Bar Cookies

When I was starting out my brand-new baking blog, I bought a cookbook that had a recipe for magic bars in it. I had no idea what a magic bar was, or what made it so magical. Did it pay my taxes for me? Find me a boyfriend? I mean, that's a pretty big statement for a cookie bar. Once I tried them, I was *hooked* (see page 76). Now I'm magically turning the bar flavors into cookies: butterscotch, chocolate, graham cracker, pecans, coconut, sweetened condensed milk, and the base. Give this fun twist a try.

18 COOKIES

INGREDIENTS

1 cup (2 sticks) butter, room temperature

1 cup brown sugar

½ cup sugar

1 egg

1 tablespoon vanilla extract

1 teaspoon baking soda

2 teaspoons cornstarch

½ teaspoon salt

2¼ cups all-purpose flour

¼ cup graham cracker crumbs

3 tablespoons sweetened condensed milk

¼ cup semi-sweet chocolate chips

¼ cup butterscotch chips

½ cup shredded coconut

½ cup chopped pecans

1. In the bowl of a stand mixer, cream together the butter and sugars until creamy and smooth, about 2 minutes. Beat in the egg and vanilla until combined. Beat in the baking soda, cornstarch, salt, and flour to combine. Lastly, beat in the graham cracker crumbs, sweetened condensed milk, chocolate chips, butterscotch chips, coconut, and pecans until combined.

2. Refrigerate the cookie dough for at least 2 hours, up to overnight. This is mandatory.

3. Preheat oven to 350 degrees F. Line 2 baking sheets with parchment paper or silicone liners. Drop rounded tablespoons of cookie dough onto the baking sheets, about 2" apart.

4. Bake for approximately 10 to 12 minutes, rotating pans halfway through baking time, until golden brown. Cookies will appear soft and a little gooey; this is normal. They'll continue to set up as they cool. Cool completely.

Crème-Filled Chocolate Chip Cookies

My family's eating habits aren't very adventurous. When it comes to food, they want what they know and love, and I can't blame them. There's something comforting in food that you grew up with; I get it. Sometimes you have to try something new, and that's what these cookies bring. They look like chocolate chip cookies but have an Oreo crème filling inside. It's gooey and sweet and the perfect surprise. **10–12 COOKIES**

INGREDIENTS

1 cup (2 sticks) butter, room temperature

1 cup brown sugar

½ cup sugar

1 egg

1 tablespoon vanilla extract

1 teaspoon baking soda

2 teaspoons cornstarch

½ teaspoon salt

2¼ cups all-purpose flour

1 cup semi-sweet chocolate chips

FOR FILLING

¼ cup vegetable shortening, room temperature

Crème filling from 10 Oreo cookies (see Note)

1 teaspoon vanilla extract

½ teaspoon salt

1½ cups powdered sugar

3 tablespoons heavy cream or milk

NOTE: Steal the crème filling from the Chocolate Mint Cookies recipe (page 106), which needs just the cookies!

1. In the bowl of a stand mixer, cream together the butter and sugars until creamy and smooth, about 2 minutes. Beat in the egg and vanilla until combined. Beat in the baking soda, cornstarch, salt, and flour to combine. Stir in the chocolate chips.

2. Refrigerate the cookie dough for at least 2 hours, up to overnight. This is mandatory.

3. While dough chills, prepare your Oreo Crème Filling. In a large bowl, beat together the shortening, crème filling, vanilla, and salt until smooth, about 2 minutes. Gradually add the powdered sugar, one cup at a time, until light and fluffy. Add in the cream 1 tablespoon at a time if mixture is too thick.

4. Drop rounded tablespoons of crème filling onto a foil-lined plate—you should have around 12. Freeze the filling balls until firm, about 1 hour.

5. Preheat oven to 350 degrees F. Line 2 baking sheets with parchment paper or silicone liners. Scoop out a heaping tablespoon of dough into your palm and flatten it slightly. Place a crème-filling ball in the middle, using your fingers to pinch the dough around the filling, enclosing it completely. Place the cookies 2" apart on the baking sheets.

6. Bake for approximately 10 to 12 minutes, rotating pans halfway through baking time, until golden brown. Cookies will appear soft and a little gooey; this is normal and they'll continue to set up as they cool. Cool completely.

Cranberry White Chip Macadamia Nut Cookies

As a teenager I'd always beg my parents to drop me off at the mall with my friends. My parents would usually give me a couple of bucks for food. I spent it all at the cookie store. They made the best, chewiest cookies around and they were worth every bite. My favorite cookie was the white chocolate macadamia nut. I combined it with my other favorite cookie—cranberry white chip—and the result is this ultra buttery, chewy cookie studded with cranberry jewels, white chips, and buttery macadamia nuts. No mall trip necessary. **18 COOKIES**

INGREDIENTS

1 cup (2 sticks) butter, room temperature

1 cup brown sugar

½ cup sugar

1 egg

1 tablespoon vanilla extract

1 teaspoon baking soda

2 teaspoons cornstarch

½ teaspoon salt

2¼ cups all-purpose flour

½ cup dried cranberries

½ cup chopped macadamia nuts

½ cup white chocolate chips

1. In the bowl of a stand mixer, cream together the butter and sugars until creamy and smooth, about 2 minutes. Beat in the egg and vanilla until combined. Beat in the baking soda, cornstarch, salt, and flour to combine. Stir in the cranberries, macadamia nuts, and white chocolate chips.

2. Refrigerate the cookie dough for at least 2 hours, up to overnight. This is mandatory.

3. Preheat oven to 350 degrees F. Line 2 baking sheets with parchment paper or silicone liners. Drop rounded tablespoons of dough onto the baking sheets, about 2" apart.

4. Bake for approximately 10 to 12 minutes, rotating pans halfway through baking time. Cookies will appear soft and a little gooey; this is normal. They'll continue to set up as they cool. Cool completely.

Frosted Cupcookies

Are you a cake person or a frosting person? I'm typically the former, but over the years I've started to indulge in lightly frosted cupcakes, frosted cookies, and maybe scraping a little extra chocolate frosting off of a layer cake. For those of you who *do* favor frosting, this is your recipe! For starters, these Frosted Cupcookies are extraordinary—they're baked in a muffin tin, resulting in a super thick, ultra fudgy cookie filled with an Oreo. Then, the entire thing is piled high with a sinfully delicious vanilla buttercream frosting that sends these over the top. You can thank me later! 12 COOKIES

INGREDIENTS

1 (24-count) package refrigerated chocolate chip cookie dough, room temperature

12 Oreo cookies

FOR TOPPING

2 batches or 1 (16-ounce) tub Vanilla Frosting (page 5)

NOTE: Try switching up the flavors in this recipe by using peanut butter cookie dough with Peanut Butter Oreos, or sugar cookie dough with Golden Oreos!

1. Preheat oven to 350 degrees F. Line a muffin pan with 12 paper liners. Set aside.

2. Take a single piece of cookie dough and flatten it slightly with the palm of your hand. Place an Oreo on top, then flatten another piece of cookie dough around the Oreo, forming a ball and completely enclosing the Oreo. Place the cookie dough ball into the muffin cup and repeat.

3. Bake the cookie cups for approximately 20 to 25 minutes or until golden brown and edges are set. Cool in the pan for about 15 minutes, then gently run a butter knife around the edge of the cookie cup to release it. Let them cool completely on a wire rack.

4. Pipe the vanilla frosting onto the cookie cups and serve. You can also spread the frosting onto the cookie cups. If you spread it on, I'd recommend making just one batch of frosting.

Peppermint Mocha Cookies

I tried my first peppermint mocha in seventh grade. It was just after Thanksgiving and my mom and I were Christmas shopping. We stopped by a coffee shop on the way to the mall and she and I both ordered one. The flavor was outstanding—creamy, smooth, milky, and swirling with that cool minty flavor. I thought I was oh-so cool carrying around a "grown up" coffee beverage. Studded with dark chocolate chunks and peppermint chips, these cookies are the perfect accompaniment to your "grown up" beverage. **16–18 COOKIES**

INGREDIENTS

1 (17.5-ounce) package double chocolate chunk cookie mix

¼ cup oil

2 tablespoons milk

1 egg

2 teaspoons espresso powder

1 teaspoon mint extract

⅔ cup peppermint baking chips

FOR TOPPING

2 squares vanilla candy coating/almond bark

⅔ cup crushed candy cane pieces

1. Preheat oven to 350 degrees F. Line 2 baking sheets with parchment paper or silicone liners. Set aside.

2. In a large bowl, combine the cookie mix, oil, milk, egg, espresso powder, and mint extract with a spatula until a soft dough has formed. Fold in the peppermint baking chips to combine.

3. Drop rounded tablespoons of dough 2" apart on the baking sheets. Bake for approximately 10 to 12 minutes, rotating pans halfway through baking time. Cool on the cookie sheets completely.

4. Melt the vanilla bark according to package directions, or until smooth. Drizzle the vanilla bark over the cookies and immediately sprinkle with the crushed candy cane pieces.

Pumpkin Candy Corn Cookies

Candy corn is a love-it-or-hate-it kind of treat. I love it! Nothing reminds me more of Halloween than candy corn. I love eating it mixed together with peanut butter chips and popcorn, but I'm always looking for new ways to use this classic candy. Putting it with pumpkin oatmeal cookies sounded like a splendid idea. The combination of the chewy oatmeal, the perfectly spiced pumpkin, and the sweet candy corn is positively irresistible. The best part? These cookies can be made super quickly with a genius shortcut so you can feed them to your trick-or-treaters in no time. **18–20 COOKIES**

INGREDIENTS

1 (14–17.5-ounce) package oatmeal
  cookie mix

1 egg

½ cup (1 stick) butter, room temperature

½ cup pumpkin purée

1 teaspoon pumpkin pie spice

½ cup all-purpose flour

¾ cup white chocolate chips

FOR TOPPING

1 cup candy corn, for topping

1. Preheat oven to 375 degrees F. Line 2 baking sheets with parchment paper or silicone liners. Set aside.

2. In a large bowl, combine the oatmeal cookie mix, egg, softened butter, pumpkin purée, pumpkin pie spice, and flour with a spatula until blended and smooth. Fold in the white chocolate chips until combined.

3. Drop rounded tablespoons of dough onto the baking sheets about 2" apart. Bake for approximately 10 to 12 minutes, rotating pans halfway through baking time, until centers appear mostly set.

4. Cool on the baking sheets for about 5 minutes, then place three candy corn pieces onto each cookie, pushing them into the cookie slightly. Cool the cookies completely on the baking sheets.

Cheesecake and Pie
Tips & Tricks

* I love using prepared graham cracker and cookie crusts for most of my pies and cheesecakes. Some recipes, like Pumpkin Spice Mini Cheesecakes and Mixed Berry Mini Cheesecakes, have homemade graham cracker crusts since they're baked in different pans. I find it's easiest to buy already ground graham cracker crumbs, but if you'd like, pulverize your own in a food processor.

* Make sure your cream cheese is room temperature before starting any recipe. To expedite this process, microwave unwrapped cream cheese on HIGH for about 20 to 30 seconds. Also, make sure your Cool Whip is thawed completely before preparing some of the pies and cheesecakes. Cool Whip needs at least four hours to thaw in the fridge.

* All of these recipes need adequate time to chill and/or set before serving, so plan accordingly!

4

Cheesecakes, Chocolate Pies, and More Creamy Treats

Mixed Berry Mini Cheesecakes

There are typically two types of people: those who like fruit in their dessert, and those who detest it. I happen to be in the former camp, because if I can eat dessert *and* have fruit, I'm clearly winning at this whole dieting thing. This cheesecake with fruit on top is one of my favorites. There's something so luscious about creamy, tangy cheesecake and tart fresh berries that scream, "Eat me as if your life depends on it." If you need a portion control excuse, I've got you covered. Just don't get mad when you eat two (or three) of these. **18 MINI CAKES**

INGREDIENTS

1 cup graham cracker crumbs

3 tablespoons brown sugar

¼ cup (½ stick) butter, melted

FOR FILLING

2 (8-ounce) packages cream cheese, room temperature

⅔ cup sugar

2 eggs

2 teaspoons vanilla extract

⅓ cup sour cream

FOR TOPPING

2 cups mixed berry pie filling, divided

Whipped cream

1½ cups fresh mixed berries

1. Preheat oven to 325 degrees F. Line 18 muffin cavities with paper liners. Set aside.

2. In a medium bowl, combine the graham cracker crumbs, brown sugar, and melted butter together until moistened. Drop a rounded tablespoon of crumb mixture into each muffin cup, pressing with the back of the measuring spoon to create a compact crust. Bake for approximately 5 to 7 minutes or until golden.

3. While crusts bake, prepare your filling. In the bowl of a stand mixer, cream together the cream cheese and sugar until soft, about 2 minutes. Add in the eggs, one at a time, and the vanilla, beating to incorporate. Lastly, beat in the sour cream until smooth.

4. Distribute the cheesecake filling evenly among the muffin cups, filling until about ¾ full. Top with a tablespoon of mixed berry filling and use a clean butter knife to swirl the cheesecake and berry filling together.

5. Bake for approximately 25 to 30 minutes or until the cheesecake appears set and puffy. Cool completely, then refrigerate for at least 2 hours.

6. To serve, top each miniature cheesecake with a dollop of whipped cream and spoon a heaping tablespoon of mixed berry pie filling on top. Top with the fresh berries. Serve immediately, and store leftovers covered in the fridge.

Banana Pudding Cheesecake

Sometimes I wish I was Southern, because Southern people have a charm about them that I'm envious of, and they can make anything sound sweet with their little accents. Plus, I love gingham and anything Cajun, which obviously makes me qualified to be Southern. I channel my inner wannabe Southern girl with this Banana Pudding Cheesecake. Just like mama used to make! SERVES 8

INGREDIENTS

2 (8-ounce) packages cream cheese, room temperature

⅔ cup sugar

2 eggs

1 teaspoon vanilla extract

2 teaspoons banana extract, optional

⅓ cup sour cream

1–2 medium ripe bananas, mashed (½ cup)

1 prepared vanilla wafer pie crust

FOR TOPPING

Whipped cream and fresh banana slices for garnish, optional

1. Preheat oven to 325 degrees F. Place the prepared pie crust onto a baking sheet and set aside.

2. In the bowl of a stand mixer, cream together the cream cheese and sugar until combined and smooth, about 2 minutes. Gradually add in the eggs one at a time, then the vanilla and banana extracts, beating until combined. Lastly, add in the sour cream and mashed bananas and cream for about 2 minutes or until completely smooth.

3. Pour the cheesecake filling into the prepared pie crust and smooth out the top. Bake for approximately 35 to 40 minutes or until the center appears set. The center may be slightly jiggly—this is okay as you don't want to over-bake. Cool the cheesecake to room temperature, then refrigerate for at least 2 hours before serving.

4. Just before serving, garnish with whipped cream and fresh banana slices, if you'd like.

Pumpkin Spice Mini Cheesecakes

When I was a little kid at Thanksgiving, I would ask for a slice of pumpkin pie with extra Cool Whip on top. I mean at *least* a half of a cup's worth—no amount was too much. I would proceed to scrape all of the Cool Whip off of the pumpkin pie slice and eat it, bite by bite, then return the piece of pumpkin pie to the table for the adults to eat. No one seemed to mind eating some little girl's pie castoff, so I got away with doing this for years. It wasn't until I was older that I realized how good pumpkin pie actually tastes. **12 MINI CAKES**

INGREDIENTS

20 gingersnap cookies, finely crushed

2 tablespoons sugar

¼ cup (½ stick) butter, melted

FOR FILLING

1 (8-ounce) package cream cheese, room temperature

½ cup brown sugar

⅔ cup pumpkin purée

1 egg

2 teaspoons vanilla extract

2 teaspoons pumpkin pie spice

1 teaspoon ground cinnamon

¼ cup sour cream

FOR TOPPING

Cool Whip or whipped cream and cinnamon sugar or additional pumpkin pie spice

1. Preheat oven to 325 degrees F. Line 12 muffin cavities with paper liners. Set aside.

2. In a medium bowl, combine the finely crushed gingersnap cookies, sugar, and melted butter until moistened. Drop heaping tablespoons of the mixture evenly into each muffin cup. Use the measuring spoon to compact the crumbs into a crust. Bake for approximately 10 to 15 minutes or until golden and set. Remove from oven but leave the oven on.

3. While crust bakes, make your cheesecake filling. In the bowl of a stand mixer, cream together the cream cheese, brown sugar, and pumpkin purée until smooth, about 2 minutes. Add in the egg, beating well, then the vanilla and spices. Lastly, beat in the sour cream.

4. Portion the cheesecake filling evenly among the muffin cups. Bake for approximately 20 to 25 minutes or until the cheesecake is set in the middle. If it's a little wiggly, that's okay—just do not over-bake. Cool the cheesecakes completely, then refrigerate for at least 3 hours or overnight until set.

5. Just before serving, peel off the paper liners and garnish with whipped cream and a dusting of cinnamon sugar or pumpkin pie spice.

Toasted Marshmallow Cheesecake

I love s'mores—the combination of gooey, toasty marshmallows, rich, melted chocolate and that crunchy, buttery graham cracker is so delicious. Most of the time I'm a traditionalist—I like 'em just the way they're meant to be. But sometimes I like to experiment with my graham cracker vessel. Instead of making a traditional crust here, I've made a Cocoa Krispy Treat crust, which elevates this no-bake cheesecake to infinity. SERVES 8–10

INGREDIENTS

6 cups Cocoa Krispies cereal

¼ cup (½ stick) butter

1 package miniature marshmallows

FOR FILLING

1 (8-ounce) package cream cheese, room temperature

¼ cup sugar

2 teaspoons vanilla extract

1 (7-ounce) jar marshmallow fluff

1 (8-ounce) package Cool Whip, thawed

FOR TOPPING

1 cup mini marshmallows, toasted (see Note)

NOTE: To toast the marshmallows, preheat your broiler and line a small baking pan with foil. Grease the foil with cooking spray and arrange the remaining 1 cup of marshmallows in an even layer. Broil for about 30 seconds to 1 minute or until toasted. You can also use a kitchen torch to the marshmallows.

1. Liberally grease a 9" springform pan with cooking spray. Set aside. Meanwhile, pour the Cocoa Krispies cereal into a large bowl.

2. In a medium saucepan, melt together the butter and marshmallows over medium-low heat, stirring constantly, until gooey and smooth. Pour this mixture over the cereal and stir to combine until the mixture is sticky and coated completely.

3. Press the coated cereal mixture into the prepared pan. Using a glass cup that's been greased on the bottom, press the cereal mixture evenly and compactly into the pan, pushing the cereal up the sides to form a crust. Allow the crust to set, about 20 minutes.

4. Meanwhile, make your cheesecake. In the bowl of a stand mixer, cream together the cream cheese, sugar, and vanilla until soft and smooth, about 2 minutes. Beat in the marshmallow fluff until combined. Lastly, fold in the Cool Whip gently until incorporated.

5. Spread the cheesecake mixture into the crust, smoothing out the top. Refrigerate for at *least* 8 hours or overnight, until set.

6. Carefully arrange the toasted marshmallows in a pile in the center of the cheesecake immediately before serving.

Carrot Cake Cheesecake Bars

There's a running joke in my family that my brother, Alex, loves carrot cake. My Grammie Pat frequently threw parties for her friends with carrot cake. When the party was over, she'd send over a slice just for Alex. I don't know why, because truth be told, he dislikes the stuff, as do my parents, my siblings, and me. However, when I made these bars, I couldn't stop eating them. The combination of the chewy, oat-y carrot cake cookie base and the smooth, velvety cheesecake sent these bars over the top. Alex may not endorse them, but I do. **9 BARS**

INGREDIENTS

2½ cups all-purpose flour

1¼ cups old-fashioned oats

1 cup brown sugar

¼ cup sugar

½ teaspoon baking soda

Pinch salt

2 teaspoons ground cinnamon

¼ teaspoon ground nutmeg

½ teaspoon ground ginger

⅛ teaspoon ground cloves

1 cup (2 sticks) butter, room temperature

½ cup finely grated carrots

½ cup shredded coconut

½ cup chopped pecans

FOR FILLING

2 (8-ounce) packages cream cheese, room temperature

⅔ cup sugar

2 teaspoons vanilla extract

2 eggs

⅓ cup sour cream

FOR TOPPING

Caramel sauce, for drizzling on top of finished bars

1. Preheat oven to 325 degrees F. Line an 8×8" or 9×9" baking pan with foil, extending the sides of the foil over the edges of the pan. Spray the foil liberally with cooking spray and set aside.

2. In the bowl of a stand mixer, add the flour, oats, brown sugar, sugar, baking soda, salt, and spices and whisk to combine. Slowly beat in the butter until a soft, tacky dough is formed. Slowly beat in the carrots, coconut, and pecans.

3. Press ¾ of the dough into the prepared pan in an even layer. Set aside remaining dough. Bake crust for approximately 15 to 20 minutes or until golden brown and the center appears set. Remove from the oven, but keep the oven on.

4. While crust bakes, prepare your cheesecake. In a clean bowl, beat the cream cheese, sugar, and vanilla until creamy and smooth, about 2 minutes. Gradually add in the eggs, one at a time, beating well after each addition. Lastly, beat in the sour cream until combined.

5. Pour the cheesecake mixture over the hot crust and smooth out the top. Crumble the remaining dough over the top.

6. Bake for approximately 30 to 40 minutes or until the cheesecake is light golden brown and the center is just barely set. Cool completely, then refrigerate for at least 2 hours. Drizzle with caramel sauce.

Black Forest Brownie Cheesecake

The day I discovered Google Translate, I spent 24 hours translating random words and phrases—usually insults—into different languages. My favorite, however, was saying nice things in German, like "Ich Lieb Dich!" (I love you) over and over at my dogs, who just looked at me like, "Oh man, another one of Hayley's tirades." Later, I discovered this quote, "Tell people you love them often, because life is short. But shout it at them in German, because life is also terrifying and confusing." What's not terrifying? These Black Forest Brownie Cheesecake Bars. Did you know Black Forest Cake is German? Now you know. **15 BARS**

INGREDIENTS

1 box chocolate fudge brownie mix

½ cup butter, melted

1 egg

FOR FILLING

2 (8-ounce) packages cream cheese, room temperature

⅔ cup sugar

2 eggs

2 teaspoons vanilla extract

⅓ cup sour cream

FOR TOPPING

1 (21-ounce) can cherry pie filling (save about ½ cup for garnish if desired)

Whipped cream, if desired

NOTE: I would recommend bringing the cheesecake to just about room temperature before serving. Once it's chilled, the brownie crust becomes very cold and somewhat hard; bringing it to just about room temperature allows it to soften.

1. Preheat oven to 325 degrees F. Line a 9×13" pan with foil, extending the sides of the foil over the edges of the pan. Spray the foil liberally with cooking spray and set aside.

2. In a large bowl, combine the brownie mix, melted butter, and egg with a spatula until combined. Dough will be thick. Press the dough evenly into the bottom of the pan.

3. In the bowl of a stand mixer, cream together the cream cheese and sugar until creamy and smooth, about 2 minutes. Gradually add in the eggs, one at a time, and the vanilla, beating well after each addition. Lastly, beat in the sour cream.

4. Pour the filling evenly over the top of the brownie crust, smoothing it out. Drop 8 to 12 heaping spoonfuls of the cherry pie filling on top of the cheesecake. Using a clean butter knife, swirl the cheesecake and cherry pie filling together.

5. Bake for approximately 25 to 30 minutes or until the cheesecake is lightly golden and the center is just about set. If it wiggles a little, that's okay—you just don't want it sloshing around in the pan. Cool completely, then refrigerate for at least 2 hours before cutting into bars to serve. Immediately before serving, top with the remaining cherry pie filling and whipped cream, if desired.

No-Bake Margarita Cheesecake Pie

My mom is my best friend, but admittedly, she's a little odd in the most lovable ways possible. For starters, the woman is allergic to cucumbers but not pickles. Cantaloupe but not watermelon. Then there's the fact that she loves anything sour and tart, but dislikes margaritas. This woman will eat a vat of hot & sour soup without so much as squinting, will suck on sour candy until her tongue swells, and puts an entire lime in her Corona—but won't touch a margarita with a ten-foot pole. To convince her to try this No-Bake Margarita Cheesecake Pie was a feat in itself, but once she did, she was hooked. It's hard not to love its refreshing lime flavor and smooth texture. Sour lovers, this one's for you! **SERVES 8**

INGREDIENTS

1 (8-ounce) package cream cheese, room temperature

1 (6-ounce) container frozen margarita mix, thawed slightly

1 (14-ounce) can sweetened condensed milk

1 (8-ounce) container Cool Whip, thawed

Juice of 1 lime

Zest of 1 lime

1 prepared graham cracker or vanilla wafer crust

FOR TOPPING

Sparkling sugar (optional)

NOTE: This pie is alcohol free! The frozen margarita mix is usually found in the frozen food aisle where the juice or fruit is located. It's free of alcohol and is merely a mixer for margaritas. If you don't like lime, feel free to make this with frozen pink lemonade, or even frozen orange juice!

1. In a large bowl, beat the cream cheese, margarita mix, and sweetened condensed milk together with an electric mixer until combined and creamy, about 2 minutes. Add in the Cool Whip, lime juice, and lime zest and continue beating for another 2 to 3 minutes or until thick and creamy. It will thicken as you whip it.

2. Pour the mixture into the prepared pie crust, smoothing out the top. Freeze for approximately 8 hours or overnight before serving. Immediately before serving, sprinkle with the coarse sparkling sugar for a "salt" appearance.

Chocolate Chip Cookie Dough Tart

I'm a big believer in celebrating pretty much everything. Got a promotion at work? Let's celebrate! It's your birthday? Let's celebrate! We survived another Monday? Celebration time! When I'm celebrating, nothing can be too extravagant, including the food. We're celebrating, so calories don't count, right? When it comes time to celebrate, I like making extraordinary desserts. This tart is one of those. It has everything you could ever want: cookie dough, ganache, cookies . . . and it comes together so easily. Feel free to try different flavors of cookie dough! SERVES 12–16

INGREDIENTS

1 (16.5-ounce) tube refrigerated chocolate chip cookie dough, at room temperature

FOR FILLING

¾ cup butter, room temperature

¾ cup brown sugar

¼ cup sugar

1 teaspoon vanilla extract

2 tablespoons milk or cream

Pinch salt

2 cups all-purpose flour

1 cup miniature semi-sweet chocolate chips

FOR TOPPING

1 (12-ounce) package semi-sweet chocolate chips

⅓ cup heavy cream

1. Preheat oven to 350 degrees F. Liberally grease a large tart pan with cooking spray.

2. Press the refrigerated cookie dough in an even layer in the tart pan. Bake for approximately 15 to 20 minutes or until golden brown and set. Cool completely.

3. While crust cools, make your cookie dough. In a large bowl, cream together the butter and sugars until creamy and smooth, about 2 minutes. Beat in the vanilla and milk to combine, then add in the salt and flour until a soft dough forms. Stir in the miniature chocolate chips.

4. Roll cookie dough into tablespoon-size balls and place on a foil-lined baking sheet. Place in the refrigerator to chill while the crust continues to cool.

5. Once crust has cooled, make your ganache. In a medium, microwave-safe bowl, melt the semi-sweet chocolate chips with the heavy cream on HIGH heat for approximately 45 seconds, stirring until melted. Pour the ganache over the cooled crust and spread in an even layer out to the edges. Immediately top with the cookie dough balls, covering the entire surface area, and cutting any dough balls to fit in the cracks.

6. Place the tart carefully onto a cookie sheet and refrigerate to set for about 20 minutes. Cut into wedges and serve! Store covered in the refrigerator.

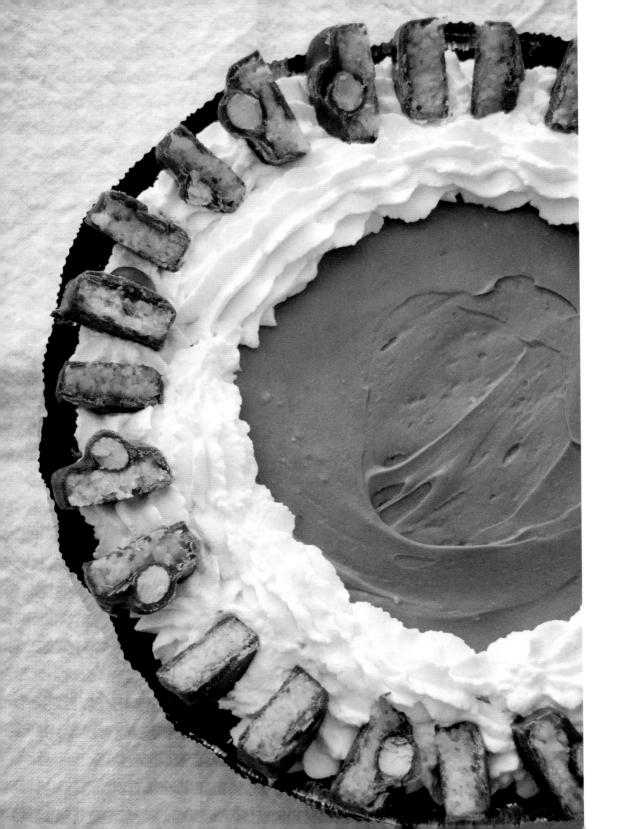

Coconut Almond Pie

On Halloween, my siblings and I would dump our loot after trick or treating and sort out candy to trade. My brother and sister always put Almond Joys in their trade pile—heathens—and I would always trade them my less favorable candy for them. My dad is also a huge Almond Joy fan, so I'd have to eat every last package so he wouldn't raid our candy bags . . . and Dad, I know you did. This pie has all the flavors in one easy, no-bake recipe! SERVES 8

INGREDIENTS

2 (8-ounce) packages cream cheese, room temperature

¾ cup powdered sugar

1 (13-ounce) jar Nutella, or chocolate hazelnut spread of your choosing

½ cup heavy whipping cream

1–2 teaspoons coconut extract (depending on how strong you like it)

1 prepared chocolate cookie crust

FOR TOPPING

½ cup heavy whipping cream

2 tablespoons sugar

8 miniature Almond Joy candy bars, unwrapped and each cut into 4 equal pieces

1. In the bowl of a stand mixer, beat the cream cheese and powdered sugar until smooth and creamy, about 2 minutes. Stir in the Nutella, ½ cup heavy whipping cream, and the coconut extract and whip on medium-high speed for about 5 to 7 minutes or until a mousse-like texture is achieved.

2. Spread the mixture into the prepared pie crust and chill in the refrigerator for about 6 to 8 hours or overnight, until set.

3. Just before serving, whip ½ cup heavy whipping cream and the sugar until stiff peaks form. Pipe onto the pie and garnish with the Almond Joy pieces.

Cookie Fluff Pie

I always feel so bad about unfriending someone or hiding their posts when it comes to social media, and I'll even whisper a little "I'm sorry" before hitting the hide button, but there are only so many political Facebook statuses or pictures of your sleeping baby I can take. I only really share desserts, so if people have a problem with dessert they *could* hide me . . . but why would anyone do that when I come up with gems like this one? This pie is a real knockout . . . one I'm perfectly happy being friends with. MAKES 1 (9-INCH) PIE

INGREDIENTS

2 (4.2-ounce) boxes instant Oreo
 pudding mix

2 cups milk

½ cup coarsely chopped Oreo cookies

1 (8-ounce) package Cool Whip, thawed

1 prepared Oreo pie crust

FOR TOPPING

Miniature Oreo cookies

Chocolate syrup

NOTE: If you cannot find the Oreo pudding mix, feel free to use instant vanilla pudding mix or white chocolate pudding mix (3.4-ounce) and proceed with the recipe as normal.

1. In a large bowl, whisk the Oreo pudding mix and the milk together until thick and creamy, about 2 minutes. Fold in the coarsely chopped Oreo cookies and the Cool Whip until completely combined and smooth.

2. Spread into the prepared pie crust and refrigerate for at least 8 hours or until firm and set. Just before serving, decorate the edge of the pie with the miniature Oreo cookies and drizzle the pie with chocolate syrup.

Root Beer Float Pie

For a really long time, I gave up soda. Diet Cola and root beer had been my faves so you can imagine it hit me pretty hard the day I realized that duh, I could no longer have root beer floats, one of my favorite summertime treats. Then one year we went to San Diego and there was a little pizza place that made their own root beer. Seeing everyone drinking a frothy glass made my mouth water, and I caved. I haven't looked back since! This pie helps me make up for all that time lost—root beer, I'll never quit you. **MAKES 1 PIE**

INGREDIENTS

¾ cup good quality root beer

½ cup milk or cream

1 (3.4-ounce) box instant vanilla pudding mix

2 tablespoons root beer concentrate

1 (8-ounce) package Cool Whip, thawed

1 prepared graham cracker or vanilla wafer pie crust

FOR TOPPING

Additional whipped cream and cherries for garnish, optional

NOTE: Don't like root beer? Substitute the root beer and root beer concentrate with orange soda and orange extract for a cool creamsicle pie! For a different flavor, try using a chocolate cookie crust.

1. In a large bowl, whisk together the root beer, milk, pudding mix, and root beer concentrate until combined and smooth, about 2 minutes or until thickened. Fold in the Cool Whip gently until completely incorporated. Make sure to get the bottom!

2. Pour the filling into the prepared pie crust and smooth out the top. Freeze for approximately 8 hours or overnight before serving. If desired, garnish with additional whipped cream and cherries.

Candy Cookie Pie

Halloween used to scare me as a kid. As I got older, I realized it wasn't as scary as real life is on a daily basis. Like the time I accidentally flashed the entire grocery store or when I told my friends I was related to catalog models and they asked my mom. Of course she said no. So Halloween isn't nearly as awful as living the remaining 364 days doing terribly humiliating things. Thankfully, I'm rewarded with candy for it. This Cookie Pie is a tribute to those silly days being scared of monsters . . . and the present days where I'm scared of myself. SERVES 8–10

INGREDIENTS

¾ cup (1½ sticks) butter, room temperature

¾ cup brown sugar

½ cup sugar

1 egg

1 tablespoon vanilla extract

1 teaspoon baking soda

2 teaspoons cornstarch

2 cups all-purpose flour

1½ cups assorted candies, roughly chopped

FOR FROSTING

¼ cup (½ stick) butter, room temperature

¼ cup cocoa powder

1 teaspoon vanilla extract

2 cups powdered sugar

3 tablespoons heavy cream or milk

FOR TOPPING

Malted milk balls and M&M's

Caramel, for drizzling

NOTE: In a hurry? This recipe can be made with a package of chocolate chip cookie mix. Just follow the directions on the back of the package.

1. Preheat oven to 350 degrees F. Liberally grease a 9" pie plate with cooking spray and place it on a rimmed baking sheet. Set aside.

2. In the bowl of a stand mixer, cream together the butter and sugars until blended and smooth, about 2 minutes. Add in the egg and vanilla, beating until combined. Lastly, add in the baking soda, cornstarch, and flour, beating slowly until a soft dough forms. Stir in the assorted chopped candies.

3. Spread the dough evenly into the prepared pie plate, smoothing out the top. Bake for approximately 25 to 30 minutes or until a toothpick inserted near the center comes out clean and the top is golden brown and set. Cool completely.

4. Once the cookie pie has cooled, prepare your frosting. In the bowl of a stand mixer, cream together the butter, cocoa, and vanilla until smooth, about 1 minute. Add in the powdered sugar, 1 cup at a time, until light and fluffy, adding in the heavy cream if frosting is too thick.

5. Pipe the frosting around the perimeter of the cookie pie and garnish with the malted milk balls and M&M's. Drizzle with caramel, if desired. Cut into wedges to serve.

Glazed Donut Pie

People often ask me where I get my inspiration, and the truth is, it comes from anywhere, at anytime, provoked by anything. If I'm not at home baking, you can usually find me pondering life choices in the candy aisle, staring mindlessly into the bags of candy thinking about recipe ideas. The inspiration for this Glazed Donut Pie happened about when I was leaving the grocery store and happened to walk by a display of donut holes. For whatever reason, I stared into the soul of those donut holes and this idea came to me like a beacon of light. I have to say, it was a pretty genius idea. SERVES 8

INGREDIENTS

1 refrigerated pie crust, room temperature

2 dozen glazed cake donut holes, cut in half

FOR FILLING

½ cup (1 stick) butter, melted

¼ cup brown sugar

1 teaspoon ground cinnamon

½ teaspoon ground nutmeg

2 eggs, lightly beaten

1 teaspoon vanilla extract

FOR GLAZE

2 tablespoons cream

1 teaspoon vanilla extract

1 cup powdered sugar

NOTE: This would work well with any cake donut hole flavor. Sometimes my local grocery store has seasonal donut hole flavors, like gingerbread or pumpkin. This would taste amazing with those, or even chocolate!

1. Preheat oven to 350 degrees F. Lightly grease a 9" pie plate with cooking spray and roll the pie crust into the pie plate, pressing to fit and crimping the edges. Pile the donut hole halves into the pie crust.

2. In a medium bowl, whisk together the melted butter, brown sugar, cinnamon, nutmeg, beaten eggs, and one teaspoon of the vanilla extract until blended. Pour this mixture over the donut holes as evenly as possible, trying to coat them all.

3. Place a pie shield (or make one with strips of foil) over the pie crust edges and bake for approximately 30 to 35 minutes or until the top is golden brown and set. Cool completely.

4. Just before serving, glaze the donut pie. In a small bowl, whisk together the cream, vanilla extract, and powdered sugar until smooth. Drizzle over the pie, and then cut into wedges to serve.

Triple Chocolate Donut Shake

I am a serious donutholic—I will eat donuts any time, for any reason, and any kind; I do not discriminate. My love for donuts stems from two likely causes—one, because my Grandma Pat or my parents would frequently take us to the local donut shop at least once a week, and two, because my mom often bought those poppable donut holes at the grocery store and we'd shovel them into our mouths like they were going out of style. We never really bought chocolate donuts, so whenever I'd get one, it was always a special treat compared to my typical sugar-yeast or cake donut. There's something so delightful about a fudgy chocolate cake donut, and they are the star in this recipe. Combined with chocolate milk, chocolate ice cream, and chocolate sauce—okay, more like quadruple chocolate—they're a heavenly treat for any donut freak! SERVES 2–4

INGREDIENTS

5 chocolate-frosted chocolate cake donuts, divided

2 cups chocolate ice cream

1–1 ½ cups chocolate milk, depending on how thick you like your shake

Chocolate syrup

Whipped cream

1. Break 3 of the chocolate donuts into rough pieces and place them in the blender along with the ice cream and milk. Blend on HIGH for 30 seconds to 1 minute or until combined and smooth, adding more milk if necessary. While milkshake blends, roughly chop the remaining two donuts into bite-size pieces.

2. Drizzle the inside of your glasses with chocolate syrup, then fill with the milkshake. Top with whipped cream and the chopped donut pieces. Serve immediately.

Copycat Pineapple Whips

I've always been a Disney girl through and through. I was fortunate enough to go to Disneyland quite frequently as a kid because my parents are also Disney people—it must be genetic. I remember going one time and only eating churros for every meal . . . middle school is a weird time in a person's life. It wasn't until fairly recently that I was exposed to the world of pineapple whips. If you haven't had one, it's a soft serve piped high on top of a pineapple mixture. The combination of that creamy vanilla soft serve with the tart, juicy pineapple is one for the books and a must-have if you go there. For those of us who can't make it to the Magic Kingdom, there's this recipe—made simple without the use of an ice cream maker. It's a little softer than the regular whip, but every bit as delicious! SERVES 2–4

INGREDIENTS

2 (20-ounce) cans crushed pineapple

3 tablespoons sugar

2–3 tablespoons lime juice

2–3 tablespoons lemon juice

1 (8-ounce) package Cool Whip, frozen

Whipped cream and cherries, optional

NOTE: This recipe will continue to harden in the freezer the longer it sits, and you'll have to chisel it out of the glass with a spoon. I recommend freezing it for only the time allowed and serving it immediately afterwards. If you don't, let it come to room temperature for about 30 to 45 minutes to soften.

1. In the blender, purée the crushed pineapple, sugar, and lime and lemon juices on HIGH for about 2 minutes. You want to break down that pineapple and make it smooth and luscious.

2. Once smooth, add in your Cool Whip. I find it's easiest to add by cutting the Cool Whip into four sections and placing the sections into the blender. Blend on HIGH until smooth and combined.

3. Pour the mixture evenly among 2 to 4 glasses (depending on the size of your glasses, of course) and freeze for at least 2 to 3 hours or until thickened. The mixture will have the consistency of a thick slushie. Just before serving, top with whipped cream and a cherry.

Pink Frosted Lemonade

My family is a fast-food family; we eat fast-food more than I care to admit. Usually it's because I don't feel like cooking that night and we're out of cereal or chicken nuggets. Seriously, our diet would make any health nut cringe in horror. One of our favorite fast-food haunts is a national chain that specializes in chicken and the employees are always super cheerful. One time, we ordered lemonade with our food, but they presented us with a thick, shake-like lemonade instead. We curiously tasted it and it turned out to be one of their frosted lemonades . . . and our new favorite drink. Sure, it's a little indulgent when dinner is chicken strips and waffle fries, but it's no different than a burger with a milkshake. I was determined to recreate this drinkable dessert at home, and this Pink Frosted Lemonade is, dare I say, even better. SERVES 2–4

INGREDIENTS

1½ cups pink lemonade

1 (12-ounce) can frozen pink or raspberry lemonade concentrate, slightly thawed

¼ cup sweetened condensed milk

1 (16-ounce) tub Cool Whip, frozen

Raspberries and lemon wedges to garnish, optional

1. In a blender, add the pink lemonade, pink lemonade concentrate, sweetened condensed milk, and Cool Whip. I like to break the Cool Whip into sections, then add the sections to the blender.

2. Blend on HIGH for about 1 minute or until smooth and creamy, stopping the blender to push the Cool Whip down if necessary.

3. Pour into glasses and garnish with raspberries and lemon wedges. Serve immediately.

Butter Pecan Ice Cream

I love to hike, but I'd never consider myself a "hiker." For one, any physical activity that doesn't involve eating or dancing in my kitchen isn't my kind of activity. Two, I'm petrified of mountain lions, which are obviously on every hiking trail in California. Hey, I've read stories. The last time I went hiking with a friend, we both got really lost—we were actually scared, running out of water, and surrounded by thorny blackberry bushes. It took us two hours to get back to civilization, and when we did, all we wanted was a cocktail . . . and some ice cream. Now any time I eat ice cream, I think of that near-death experience and am reminded of how lucky I am . . . and how if I avoid hiking, I can eat ice cream any time I want, especially since this recipe doesn't require an ice cream maker! SERVES 6–8

INGREDIENTS

2 cups very cold heavy cream

1 teaspoon vanilla extract

1 teaspoon butter extract

1 (14-ounce) can sweetened condensed milk

1 cup candied pecans, roughly chopped

1 cup toffee bits

1 cup caramel sauce or dulce de leche

1. In the bowl of a stand mixer, whip the heavy cream on HIGH until stiff peaks form, about 5 to 7 minutes. Once whipped and stiff, beat in the vanilla and butter extracts to combine.

2. Fold the sweetened condensed milk into the whipped cream very gently, then lightly stir in the chopped candied pecans and toffee bits.

3. Pour half of the mixture into a freezer-safe large bowl with a lid. Drizzle with half of the caramel sauce. Top with the remaining ice cream, then drizzle with the remaining caramel sauce.

4. Freeze for at least 8 hours or overnight, until firm.

Lemon Lush Dessert

It may be hard to believe, but I consider myself pretty low maintenance. I don't need to be swooned with roses and champagne—I'd be fine going to the hole-in-the-wall Chinese place for takeout. Most days I don't even wear makeup, and I wear clothes that could be considered "possible pajamas." Although I may take a low-key approach, my platinum blonde hair is, of course, the most high-maintenance hair anyone could have. C'est la vie. My laid-back lifestyle also extends to my baking—I don't want to have to spend hours in the kitchen slaving over a tasty dessert when I can take shortcuts to make an equally scrumptious one in minutes. While this recipe needs time to set up in the fridge, it's such a cinch to make and comes together quickly. That lemon flavor is the real winner here! SERVES 9

INGREDIENTS
20 Lemon Oreos

¼ cup (½ stick) butter, melted

FOR FILLING
1 (3.4-ounce) box instant lemon pudding mix

1 cup milk

Zest of 1 lemon

1 (8-ounce) tub Cool Whip, thawed and divided

FOR TOPPING
16 Lemon Oreos

NOTE: This recipe can be made a number of different ways: use regular Oreos and chocolate pudding or mint Oreos and chocolate pudding with a teaspoon of mint extract added!

1. Lightly grease an 8×8" or 9×9" square baking pan with cooking spray. Set aside briefly.

2. In a gallon-size resealable plastic bag, place 20 Oreos. Using a meat mallet or rolling pin, crush the cookies until they're coarse crumbs. Pour them into a bowl with the melted butter and toss to combine. Press the mixture into the bottom of the prepared baking pan in an even layer, as compact as possible. Set aside.

3. Clean out the bowl and whisk together the pudding mix, milk, and lemon zest for 2 minutes or until thickened and combined. Fold in ½ cup Cool Whip until combined. Spread into the prepared pan. Top with the remaining package of Cool Whip and spread to cover.

4. Place the remaining Oreos into the same plastic bag and coarsely crush them. Sprinkle the crushed Oreos over the top. Refrigerate until set, about 6 hours.

Strawberry Pretzel Salad Parfaits

Have you ever heard of Strawberry Pretzel Salad? Don't worry, folks—this isn't a typical salad made with greens and croutons. This kind of salad boasts juicy, ripe strawberries, a fluffy whipped cream cheese, and salty, crunchy pretzels. Normally it's made in a pan, but who can resist perfectly portion-size parfaits? Believe me, after one bite, you may never go back to conventional salads. MAKES 2–4 PARFAITS

INGREDIENTS

1 (12-ounce) bag pretzels, coarsely crushed (about 2½ cups)

2 tablespoons sugar

¼ cup butter, melted

FOR FILLING

2 (8-ounce) packages cream cheese, room temperature

½ cup sugar

1 teaspoon vanilla extract

1 (8-ounce) tub Cool Whip, thawed

FOR TOPPING

1 cup chopped strawberries

1. First, make your crust. In a medium bowl, combine the coarsely crushed pretzels with the sugar and melted butter until moistened. Distribute the mixture evenly among 2 to 4 parfait glasses or trifles. The size of your parfait will depend on how large your glasses are.

2. Make the filling: In a large bowl, beat together the cream cheese, sugar, and vanilla extract with a handheld electric mixer on medium speed, about 2 minutes. Fold in the Cool Whip until completely combined and fluffy. Spoon the cheesecake mixture into a large resealable plastic bag, seal out the air, and snip off a tip of the bag.

3. Pipe the cheesecake about halfway full into the jars. Sprinkle with about 2 to 3 tablespoons chopped strawberries. Continue piping the mixture until it reaches the brim of the jar and top with another 2 to 3 tablespoons of chopped strawberries. Repeat with remaining jars.

4. Serve immediately, or store leftovers in the fridge for 1 day.

Brownie Bombs and
Candy-licious Confections

Brownie Bomb
Tips & Tricks

* When I make Brownie Bombs, I always use a brownie mix to make things easier. Make sure your brownies are ultra fudgy—the package should say "Fudge Brownie," "Chocolate Fudge," or "Ultimate Fudge" (you get the idea). Get the "9 x 13 Family Size" box—it's usually about 18 ounces. Then make sure you follow the directions for fudgy brownies (not cakey) on the box and use a light-colored or glass pan. Generally, I bake mine for about 20 to 22 minutes until a toothpick inserted near the center comes out with moist crumbs. Don't mistake fudgy with underbaked, because a goopy brownie (while delicious) won't make a decent bomb. The fudgy brownies are tackier, making them easier to conform around the filling and stick together.

* The brownies for Brownie Bombs are made in a 9 × 13" baking pan. I recommend cutting the brownies into 15 equal pieces, and I *highly* recommend trimming the edges off of the brownies. The tougher, crispier edges are great for snacking, but don't make it easy to roll into balls. Trim the edges first, then cut the brownies.

* Freezing the filling is essential for making Brownie Bombs! Make sure your cookie dough or whatever filling you may be using is thoroughly firm and solid before wrapping it in the brownie. Otherwise, the filling will gush out all over the place and make a mess.

* Don't get hung up on your bombs looking perfect. A good handful of my Brownie Bombs aren't completely covered with brownie—and that's okay! If a bit of cookie dough is peeking out from under the brownie layer, no worries. I've never known anyone offended by a little cookie dough peep show ☺.

* ***The Great Doughbate:*** Many people believe that eating raw cookie dough is dangerous, due to the raw eggs in most prepared cookie dough recipes. While I have personally had no issues eating raw cookie dough, both prepared from scratch and packaged, I know this may not be the case for everyone. These cookie dough recipes in the book are purposefully made *egg-free* so your worries of contracting salmonella and growing a third eyeball are eliminated. *However,* at your own discretion, feel free to substitute premade refrigerated cookie dough in a pinch. Just don't blame me if you grow a third eyeball.

Coating Your
Brownie Bombs

1. Use a clean bowl to melt your chocolate. Chocolate is very prone to seizing, and one of the biggest causes is water. If your bowl has even the littlest droplet of water in it, the chocolate could thicken or harden during the melting process and result in a dense paste, rendering it absolutely unusable. Make sure whenever you're working with chocolate or almond bark that your bowls and utensils are wiped clean and dry!

2. Before coating the bombs in their chocolate blanket, make sure they're thoroughly solid, too. This helps the chocolate layer smother the cold bomb quicker *and* helps it set faster, too. Faster setting leads to quicker eating. Just sayin'.

3. Because your bombs are cold and the chocolate is hot, that also means working quickly is essential. Work with only one bomb at a time—dip it and, if necessary, garnish with the sprinkles/chips/what-have-you immediately afterward. The chocolate will harden quite fast and you'll need to be prepared to garnish immediately!

4. My favorite tool to dip is one you use regularly in the kitchen: a fork! Drop the Brownie Bomb into the melted chocolate and use the fork to swirl the chocolate around the bomb to coat it thoroughly. Gently slide the tines of the fork underneath the bomb and allow any excess chocolate to drip off of the bomb and back into the bowl. Then carefully slide the slick bomb off of the fork's tines and onto your prepared baking sheet. Easy peasy!

Chocolate Chip Cookie Dough Brownie Bombs

Back in 2012, I was 21 years old. I was one year into writing my blog, had just discovered yoga pants, and was driving the world's crappiest car. I also invented the Internet's favorite treat in the history of ever (slight exaggeration), the Chocolate Chip Cookie Dough Brownie Bomb. How did the world not already have a decadent, egg-free chocolate chip cookie dough ball wrapped in a fudgy brownie and coated in rich chocolate yet? How did I, someone who wears tutus regularly and sings Spice Girls off-key, manage to invent something so delicious and infamous? Like what happens in the Bermuda Triangle, whether or not aliens exist, and why they sell bikinis in January, some things we'll just never know. **15 BOMBS**

INGREDIENTS

½ cup (1 stick) butter, room temperature

½ cup light brown sugar, packed

¼ cup granulated white sugar

2 tablespoons milk

1 tablespoon vanilla extract

1¾ cups all-purpose flour

Pinch salt

1 cup miniature chocolate chips

1 (9×13" pan) fudge brownies, baked, cooled, and cut into 15 equal squares

FOR TOPPING

1 (16-ounce) package chocolate candy coating/chocolate almond bark

½ cup miniature chocolate chips

NOTE: The bombs are best enjoyed within 2 to 3 days of their creation. Store leftover bombs in an airtight container in the fridge or freezer.

1. In the bowl of a stand mixer affixed with the paddle attachment, combine the butter and sugars until creamy, about 2 minutes. Beat in the milk and vanilla extract. Lastly, beat in the flour and salt until a soft dough has formed. Stir in 1 cup of the miniature chocolate chips, reserving the remaining ½ cup for the topping.

2. Using your cookie dough scoop, portion tablespoon-size balls of cookie dough onto a foil or silicone lined baking sheet. You should have roughly 15 balls of dough. Freeze the dough balls for about 30 minutes to an hour, or until firm.

3. Take a square of brownie and gently flatten it in the palm of your hand by pressing both of your hands together. Wrap the flattened brownie around the cookie dough ball so the shiny side of the brownie is directly touching the dough ball. Begin pinching and rolling the brownie in your hands so the brownie coats the cookie dough ball as evenly as possible. If the brownie does not completely cover the cookie dough ball, that's okay—everything will be covered in chocolate shortly. However, try your

best to enclose the dough ball with the brownie. Return the brownie bombs to the same sheet and repeat with remaining bombs. Freeze the bombs for about 20 to 30 minutes to firm.

4. Melt your chocolate bark according to package directions, or until smooth. Dip the brownie bombs into the melted chocolate (see page 167). Return the coated bomb to the baking sheet; immediately sprinkle with a generous pinch of reserved miniature chocolate chips. Repeat with remaining bombs, and eat!

Rocky Road Cookie Dough Brownie Bombs

Growing up, my dad taught me many important life lessons. One: Always aim for the throat when attacking someone. Two: Watch *The Simpsons* religiously. Three: Ice cream is one of the best desserts. His favorite has always been rocky road. Rocky road comprises everything I love: gooey marshmallows, salty pecans, and chocolate. Dad, these bombs are for you! Let's eat them in the company of America's favorite cartoon family. **15 BOMBS**

INGREDIENTS

½ cup (1 stick) butter, room temperature

½ cup light brown sugar, packed

¼ cup granulated white sugar

2 tablespoons milk

1 tablespoon vanilla extract

1¾ cups all-purpose flour

Pinch salt

½ cup chopped pecans

½ cup miniature marshmallow bits

1 (9×13" pan) fudgy brownies, baked, cooled, and cut into 15 equal squares

FOR TOPPING

1 (16-ounce) package chocolate candy coating/chocolate almond bark

½ cup miniature mashmallow bits

½ cup chopped pecans

1. In the bowl of a stand mixer affixed with the paddle attachment, combine the butter and sugars until creamy, about 2 minutes. Beat in the milk and vanilla extract. Lastly, beat in the flour and salt until a soft dough has formed. Stir in ½ cup of chopped pecans and ½ cup of marshmallow bits until combined.

2. Using your cookie dough scoop, portion tablespoon-size balls of cookie dough onto a foil or silicone lined baking sheet. You should have roughly 15 balls of dough. Freeze the dough balls for about 30 minutes to an hour, or until firm.

3. Take a square of brownie and gently flatten it in the palm of your hand by pressing both of your hands together. Wrap the flattened brownie around the cookie dough ball so the shiny side of the brownie is directly touching the dough ball. Begin pinching and rolling the brownie in your hands so the brownie coats the cookie dough ball as evenly as possible. If the brownie does not completely cover the cookie dough ball, that's okay—everything will be covered in chocolate shortly. However, try your best to enclose the dough ball with the brownie. Return the brownie bombs to the same sheet and repeat with remaining bombs. Freeze the bombs for about 20 to 30 minutes to firm.

4. Melt your chocolate bark according to package directions, or until smooth. Dip the brownie bombs into the melted chocolate (see page 167). Return the coated bomb to the baking sheet; immediately sprinkle with a generous pinch of reserved miniature marshmallow bits and chopped pecans. Allow to set, then eat!

Cheesecake Brownie Bombs

Cheesecake is one of those desserts that I usually (regrettably) forget about. That is, until I remember cheesecake exists and then my world begins circling again. Not to get all *Forrest Gump* on you, but there's original cheesecake, strawberry cheesecake, turtle cheesecake, chocolate cheesecake, carrot cake cheesecake, Oreo cheesecake, red velvet cheesecake, chocolate mint cheesecake . . . and about 18,458 additional flavors. However, for these bombs I'm using regular ol' cheesecake bites that you can find in the freezer section of most grocery stores. Feel free to substitute a flavored cheesecake if you're feeling frisky. **15 BOMBS**

INGREDIENTS

1 (9×13) pan fudge brownies, baked, cooled, and cut into 15 squares

15 pieces frozen bite-size cheesecake (see Note)

FOR TOPPING

1 (16-ounce) package chocolate candy coating/chocolate almond bark

½ cup crushed honey graham crackers (about 3 crackers)

NOTE: Most grocery stores carry bite-size cheesecake pieces in the freezer section, which is exactly what I use for this recipe. Sometimes the cheesecake is plain, other times it's chocolate-coated or flavored—any type of cheesecake will work just fine. If you cannot find bite-size cheesecake pieces, feel free to scoop individual tablespoon-size balls of actual cheesecake and freeze the pieces before using.

1. Line a baking sheet with foil or a silicone liner. Set aside. Take a square of brownie and gently flatten it in the palm of your hand by pressing both of your hands together. Wrap the flattened brownie around the frozen cheesecake bite so the shiny side of the brownie is directly touching the cheesecake. Begin pinching and rolling the brownie in your hands so the brownie coats the cheesecake bite as evenly as possible. If the brownie does not completely cover the cheesecake bite, that's okay—everything will be covered in chocolate shortly. However, try your best to enclose the cheesecake with the brownie. Return the brownie bomb to the same sheet and repeat with remaining bomb. Freeze the bombs for about 20 to 30 minutes to firm.

2. Melt your chocolate bark according to package directions, or until smooth. Dip the brownie bombs into the melted chocolate (see page 167). Return the coated bomb to the baking sheet; immediately sprinkle with a generous pinch of the graham cracker crumbs. Repeat with remaining bombs, and eat!

3. These Cheesecake Brownie Bombs are best served immediately or 2 to 3 days after their creation. Store leftover bombs in the fridge or freezer.

Vanilla Cupcake Brownie Bombs

Back in the day, I worked at a cupcake shop when cupcake shops were actually relevant. While I loved working there, it was so hard for me to resist fat, fluffy, fresh-baked cupcakes every single day. In addition, the fact that our shop only played one type of music made me want to bury my head in the giant vat of frosting. If you've ever been subjected to listening to the same artist over and over *and* have tried to resist sugary cupcakes, it isn't an easy task—and at times, I caved. Anytime I broke my stride, I always headed for the vanilla cupcake. A classic for a reason, and that's what is stuffed in these outrageous sugar bombs. **15 BOMBS**

INGREDIENTS

15 miniature frosted vanilla cupcakes (from your favorite bakery, or homemade), frozen until solid

1 (9×13") pan fudgy brownies, baked, cooled and cut into 15 squares

FOR TOPPING

1 (16-ounce) package vanilla candy coating/vanilla almond bark

1 batch Vanilla Frosting (recipe on page 5)

Rainbow sprinkles

1. Line a baking sheet with foil or a silicone liner. Set aside. Remove the wrappers from the frozen miniature cupcakes; discard wrappers. Take a square of brownie and gently flatten it in the palm of your hand by pressing both of your hands together. Wrap the flattened brownie around the frozen vanilla cupcake. Begin pinching and rolling the brownie in your hands so the brownie coats the cupcake as evenly as possible. If the brownie does not completely cover the cupcake, that's okay—everything will be covered in chocolate shortly. However, try your best to enclose the cupcake with the brownie. Return the brownie bombs to the same sheet and repeat with remaining bombs. Freeze the bombs for about 20 to 30 minutes to firm.

2. Melt your white chocolate bark according to package directions, or until smooth. Dip the brownie bombs into the melted white chocolate (see page 167). Return the coated bomb to the baking sheet and allow the white chocolate to set.

3. Spoon the icing into a disposable piping bag affixed with a large, open-star tip. Pipe the frosting high onto each brownie bomb, then garnish with rainbow sprinkles. Serve the brownie bombs immediately, or store leftovers in the fridge covered in an airtight container.

Coconut Almond Brownie Bombs

People ask me all the time how it's possible that I don't have cavities or weigh a ton. It's about moderation . . . and whether or not that dessert has coconut in it—in which case, I'll inhale it all. These Coconut Almond Brownie Bombs taste just like Almond Joys but they're super fudgy and come in pre-made portion control. For that, my waist-line and I are very glad. 15 BOMBS

INGREDIENTS

2 cups shredded coconut

¾ cup sweetened condensed milk

1 cup powdered sugar

15 whole almonds

1 (9×13) pan fudgy brownies, baked, cooled, and cut into 15 squares

FOR TOPPING

1 (16-ounce) package chocolate candy coating/chocolate almond bark

1 square vanilla candy coating/vanilla almond bark

NOTE: Don't like almonds? Feel free to omit them from this recipe for an instant Mounds Brownie Bomb.

1. To make your coconut filling, stir together the shredded coconut, sweetened condensed milk, and the powdered sugar in a large bowl until the filling is moist enough to mold into balls but not too wet. Add more powdered sugar if it's too wet.

2. Using a cookie dough scoop, portion the coconut mixture into heaping, rounded tablespoons and place them onto a foil- or silicone-lined baking sheet. Top each coconut ball with a single whole almond. Freeze the mixture until firm, about 30 minutes.

3. Take a square of brownie and gently flatten it in the palm of your hand by pressing both of your hands together. Wrap the flattened brownie around the frozen coconut ball. Begin pinching and rolling the brownie in your hands so the brownie coats the frosting ball as evenly as possible. If the brownie does not completely cover the coconut ball, that's okay—everything will be covered in chocolate shortly. However, try your best to enclose the coconut ball with the brownie. Return the brownie bombs to the same sheet and repeat with remaining bombs. Freeze the bombs for about 20 to 30 minutes to firm.

4. Melt your chocolate bark according to package directions, or until smooth. Dip the brownie bombs into the melted chocolate (see page 167). Return the coated bomb to the baking sheet and let set. Once set, melt the vanilla almond bark until smooth and place it into a small, resealable plastic bag. Snip off a corner of the bag and drizzle the melted vanilla almond bark onto the tops of the brownie bombs. Allow the vanilla almond bark to set, then serve.

S'mores Cookie Dough Brownie Bombs

I've always hated camping. Unless there's WiFi, a comfy bed, a hot shower, a toilet, and room service, I'm not interested in lying on the ground like a cavewoman. However, I do love me some s'mores and believe they don't have to be associated with camping. S'mores can totally be an everyday activity. I'm here to take back the s'more, and I hope you'll join me! Together, we'll eat S'mores Cookie Dough Brownie Bombs in our hotel room beds. With fluffy robes, obviously. **15 BOMBS**

INGREDIENTS

½ cup (1 stick) butter, room temperature

½ cup light brown sugar, packed

¼ cup granulated white sugar

2 tablespoons milk

1 tablespoon vanilla extract

1¾ cups all-purpose flour

Pinch salt

1 cup miniature chocolate chips

½ cup miniature marshmallow bits (see Note)

1 (9×13" pan) fudgy brownies, baked, cooled, and cut into 15 equal squares

FOR TOPPING

1 (16-ounce) package chocolate candy coating/chocolate almond bark

½ cup miniature marshmallow bits

½ cup graham cracker crumbs, finely crushed

NOTE: Marshmallow Bits are made by Jet-Puffed Marshmallows and are typically found in the baking aisle, or sometimes near the hot chocolate section. They're like freeze-dried miniature marshmallows, similar in taste and texture to that of marshmallow cereal. They're perfect for this recipe since they aren't soft and squishy like your typical marshmallows.

1. In the bowl of a stand mixer affixed with the paddle attachment, combine the butter and sugars until creamy, about 2 minutes. Beat in the milk and vanilla extract. Lastly, beat in the flour and salt until a soft dough has formed. Stir in the miniature chocolate chips and ½ cup of miniature marshmallow bits.

2. Using your cookie dough scoop, portion tablespoon-size balls of cookie dough onto a foil or silicone-lined baking sheet. You should have roughly 15 balls of dough. Freeze the dough balls for about 30 minutes to an hour, or until firm.

3. Take a square of brownie and gently flatten it in the palm of your hand by pressing both of your hands together. Wrap the flattened brownie around the cookie dough ball so the shiny side of the brownie is directly touching the dough ball. Begin pinching and rolling the brownie in your hands so the brownie coats the cookie dough ball as evenly as possible. If the brownie does not completely cover the cookie dough ball, that's okay—everything will be covered in chocolate shortly. However, try your best to enclose the dough ball with the brownie. Return the brownie bomb to the same sheet and repeat with remaining bombs. Freeze the bombs for about 20 to 30 minutes to firm.

4. Melt your chocolate bark according to package directions, or until smooth. Dip the brownie bombs into the melted chocolate (see page 167). Return the coated bomb to the baking sheet; immediately sprinkle with a generous pinch of miniature marshmallow bits and some of the crushed graham cracker crumbs. Repeat with remaining bombs, and eat!

Chocolate-Walnut Fudge Brownie Bombs

Every time I go to the mall, I visit See's Candies to grab a square of fudge. If you've never been there, it's a small, quaint, black-and-white bakery filled to the brim with chocolate, fudge, and other assorted candies that are all made here in California. Their basic chocolate-walnut fudge totally satisfies the old woman who lives in my soul and forces me to go to bed at 8 pm. My brownie bombs have actual pieces of See's fudge inside of them, but if you don't have See's, use another brand of basic fudge. Beware: Even the craziest chocoholics I have met said these bombs were rich. You've been warned! **15 BOMBS**

INGREDIENTS

1 (9×13") pan fudgy brownies, baked, cooled, and cut into 15 (2-inch) pieces

15 (1-inch) squares of chocolate-walnut fudge (see Note)

FOR TOPPING

1 (16-ounce) package chocolate candy coating/chocolate almond bark

½ cup chopped walnuts

NOTE: Don't like your fudge with nuts? Use a nut-free fudge for allergies or personal preferences. White fudge or caramel fudge would also be great here!

1. Line a rimmed baking sheet with foil and set aside. Meanwhile, gently flatten each brownie square in the palm of your hand. Wrap the flattened brownie around a piece of fudge. Begin pinching and rolling the brownie in your hands so the brownie coats the fudge as evenly as possible. If the brownie does not completely cover fudge, that's okay—everything will be covered in chocolate shortly. However, try your best to enclose the fudge with the brownie. Return the brownie bomb to the same sheet and repeat with remaining bombs. Freeze the bombs for about 20 to 30 minutes to firm.

2. Melt your chocolate almond bark according to package directions, or until smooth, then stir in the coconut extract quickly. Dip the brownie bombs into the melted chocolate (see page 167). Return the coated bomb to the baking sheet, and sprinkle the tops with the chopped walnuts. Allow the bombs to set before serving!

Baklava Brownie Bombs

I hate to admit it, but I'm kind of a bad traveler. If I'm not at least two hours early to a flight, I begin to have a mild panic attack. If I can't get an aisle seat—honey, you better watch out. I really dislike being a diva, but that's what happens when your natural state is what others consider "high anxiety." Of all the times I've traveled, there was one time where there were no problems. It was like a miracle—granted, it was only to Southern California, which is about a 30 minute flight . . . but still! When I deplaned, I went straight to the hotel and next door was a baklava place with the best baklava. If I could be rewarded with baklava at the end of every flight, maybe I wouldn't be such a bad traveler. SERVES 12

INGREDIENTS

1 (9×13") pan fudgy brownies, baked, cooled, and cut into 12 equal pieces

12 (1–2") pieces of baklava (any kind), frozen

FOR TOPPING

1 (16-ounce) package vanilla candy coating/almond bark

¾ cup toffee bits

½ cup golden sugar sprinkles

1. Take a square of brownie and gently flatten it in the palm of your hand by pressing both of your hands together. Wrap the flattened brownie around the frozen baklava so the shiny side of the brownie is directly touching the baklava. Begin pinching and rolling the brownie in your hands so the brownie coats the baklava as evenly as possible. If the brownie does not completely cover the baklava, that's okay—everything will be covered in chocolate shortly. However, try your best to enclose the baklava with the brownie. Return the brownie bomb to the same sheet and repeat with remaining bombs. Freeze the bombs for about 20 to 30 minutes to firm.

2. Melt your vanilla almond bark according to package directions, or until smooth. Dip the brownie bombs into the melted vanilla almond bark (see page 167). Return the coated bomb to the baking sheet; immediately sprinkle with a generous pinch of toffee bits and gold sprinkles. Allow to set before eating.

Peanut Butter Cookie Dough Brownie Bombs

Once I created the original Brownie Bomb, I couldn't help but create multiple cookie dough-flavored bombs. As you've read already, there's s'mores, rocky road, and now Peanut Butter Cookie Dough, which may be my family's favorite of the bunch. It's no surprise—this particular flavor tastes like the center of a peanut butter cup and has the most luscious white chocolate peanut butter coating around it. If you're a peanut butter fanatic like my mom and sister, you'll want to top these with peanut butter chips or peanut butter candies. **15 BOMBS**

INGREDIENTS

½ cup (1 stick) butter, room temperature

⅓ cup creamy peanut butter

½ cup brown sugar

¼ cup sugar

2 teaspoons milk

1 teaspoon vanilla extract

2 cups all-purpose flour

Pinch salt

1 (9×13") pan fudgy brownies, baked, cooled, and cut into 15 equal pieces

FOR TOPPING

1 (16-ounce) package vanilla candy coating/almond bark

2 tablespoons creamy peanut butter

¾ cup peanut butter chips or chopped peanut butter candies

NOTE: This cookie dough recipe yields more cookie dough balls than the other ones. Freeze the extras for when a cookie dough craving strikes, crumble them on top of ice cream, blend them into a milkshake, or coat the cookie dough balls with melted chocolate.

1. In the bowl of a stand mixer affixed with the paddle attachment, combine the butter, ⅓ cup of the peanut butter, and sugars until creamy, about 2 minutes. Beat in the milk and vanilla extract. Lastly, beat in the flour and salt until a soft dough has formed.

2. Using your cookie dough scoop, portion tablespoon-size balls of cookie dough onto a foil or silicone-lined baking sheet. You should have roughly 15 balls of dough. Freeze the dough balls for about 30 minutes to an hour, or until firm.

3. Take a square of brownie and gently flatten it in the palm of your hand by pressing both of your hands together. Wrap the flattened brownie around the cookie dough ball so the shiny side of the brownie is directly touching the dough ball. Begin pinching and rolling the brownie in your hands so the brownie coats the cookie dough ball as evenly as possible. If the brownie does not completely cover the cookie dough ball, that's okay—everything will be covered in chocolate shortly. However, try your best to enclose the dough ball with the brownie. Return the brownie bombs to the same sheet and repeat with remaining bombs. Freeze the bombs for about 20 to 30 minutes to firm.

4. Melt your vanilla almond bark with the peanut butter according to package directions, or until smooth. Dip the brownie bombs into the melted white chocolate (see page 167). Return the coated bomb to the baking sheet; immediately sprinkle with a generous pinch of peanut butter chips or peanut butter candies. Allow to set before serving.

Red Velvet Truffle Brownie Bombs

After visiting Austin, Texas, I started using the term "y'all" quite a bit, wanted a pair of cowgirl boots, and was craving fried chicken more than any normal person should. I fell in love with the Southern charm and the Austin quirkiness, but my hair could do without the humidity. One thing I noticed while on a bakery tour was red velvet cake. Boy was it delicious, and it was the inspiration for these Red Velvet Truffle Brownie Bombs. All that's missing is the Southern accent. **15 BOMBS**

INGREDIENTS

1¼ cups red velvet cake mix

⅓ cup all-purpose flour

⅓ cup sugar

⅓ cup melted butter

1 teaspoon vanilla extract

1–2 tablespoons heavy cream or milk

1 (9×13") pan fudgy brownies, baked, cooled, and cut into 15 equal pieces

FOR TOPPING

1 (16-ounce) package vanilla candy coating/almond bark

2 squares chocolate candy coating/ almond bark

1. Line a baking sheet with foil and set aside. In a large bowl, whisk together the cake mix, flour, and sugar. Add in the melted butter, vanilla extract, and one tablespoon of cream until blended. If mixture is super thick, add in the remaining tablespoon of cream.

2. Drop rounded tablespoons of the mixture onto the prepared pan. You should have about 15 truffles. Freeze the truffles until firm, about 20 to 30 minutes.

3. Once truffles are firm, take a square of brownie and gently flatten it in the palm of your hand by pressing both of your hands together. Wrap the flattened brownie around the truffle so the shiny side of the brownie is directly touching the truffle. Begin pinching and rolling the brownie in your hands so the brownie coats the truffle as evenly as possible. If the brownie does not completely cover the truffle, that's okay—everything will be covered in chocolate shortly. Return the brownie bombs to the same sheet and repeat with remaining bombs. Freeze the bombs for about 20 to 30 minutes to firm.

4. Melt your vanilla almond bark according to package directions, or until smooth. Dip the brownie bombs into the melted white chocolate (see page 167). Return the coated bomb to the baking sheet and let set for about 10 minutes.

5. Once set, melt the squares of chocolate almond bark in a small bowl. Pour the melted chocolate into a sandwich bag, seal out the air and snip off a corner of the bag. Drizzle the chocolate over the brownie bombs. Let the chocolate set, then serve.

Easy Almond Roca

I'm a big, fat scaredy cat; I'm creeped out and afraid of so many random—usually irrational—things. Things like mountain lions (nope), heights (heck nope), and being home alone when someone rings the doorbell (yikes). Another one of my random fears includes candy thermometers. I don't know why, but there's something so intimidating about them that it prevents me from making lots of yummy homemade candy. Thankfully, this recipe for Homemade Almond Roca does not require a thermometer—unheard of when you're making homemade toffee. I promise, it's every bit as authentic as a thermometer'd recipe. SERVES 6–8

INGREDIENTS

1–1½ cups coarsely chopped almond pieces

1 cup (2 sticks) butter

1 cup sugar

1 teaspoon vanilla extract

1 cup semi-sweet chocolate chips

1. Line an 8×8" or 9×9" pan with foil, extending the sides of the foil over the edges of the pan. Mist the foil very lightly with the cooking spray. Sprinkle ½ to ¾ cup almond pieces evenly over the bottom of the pan and set aside.

2. In a medium saucepan, melt the butter and sugar together over medium-high heat, stirring constantly. Bring the mixture to a boil, stirring constantly, for about 7 to 10 minutes, or until the mixture is thick and caramel colored. The color will look almost like a raw almond. Once it reaches this color, immediately pull it from the heat and whisk in the vanilla.

3. Pour the toffee mixture immediately over the almond pieces, smoothing to fit the pan. The pan will be VERY hot, so be careful! Let the toffee set for about 2 to 3 minutes, then sprinkle the top evenly with the chocolate chips. Let stand for about 5 minutes, then use an offset spatula to spread the chocolate evenly over the top. Immediately sprinkle with the remaining ½ to ¾ cup almond pieces.

4. Allow the toffee to set at room temperature for about 6 hours, or 3 to 4 hours in the fridge before breaking into pieces. Please note that if the toffee is cold, the chocolate layer is more likely to separate from the toffee layer, so I recommend bringing any cold toffee to room temperature before breaking into pieces.

2 (or 3) Ingredient Fudge

We had this wonderful neighbor growing up named Sue. Sue was the sweetest lady—on every holiday, we'd wake up and run to our mailbox to find three perfectly packaged treat bags—one for me and my siblings. Inside each package was a kid's dream—cool pencils and stickers, temporary tattoos, little bouncy balls, and *always* a mini box of chocolates. The chocolates usually had a piece of fudge in them, and that was the piece I went for first. It started my love of fudge from a very early age, and I attribute that—and my affinity for boxed chocolates—to Sue. This fudge is so fool-proof, any novice baker can make it with ease. It has only two ingredients—three if you count walnuts—and is such a cinch to make. This one's for you, Sue! SERVES 20–24

INGREDIENTS

1 (12-ounce) bag semi-sweet chocolate chips

1 (16-ounce) can chocolate frosting

1 cup chopped walnuts, optional

1. Line an 8×8" or 9×9" pan with foil, extending the sides of the foil over the edges of the pan. Mist the foil lightly with cooking spray. Set aside.

2. Add the chocolate chips to a large, clean bowl and microwave on HIGH power for 45 seconds. Stir until melted, then fold in the chocolate frosting until combined. Mixture will be quite thick. At this point, stir in your chopped walnuts, if using.

3. Spread the mixture into the prepared pan, trying your best to smooth out the top. Refrigerate for 2 hours or until firm, then cut into squares to serve.

Maple Bacon Pecan Baklava

I worked in a cupcake shop where we had a maple bacon cupcake before the world went bonkers over bacon product in desserts. The cupcake was especially popular with our male customers, like my dad, who loved when I brought them home. When I was developing recipes for this book, I had to make a total "dude food" recipe, and folks, this is it. It's gooey, sticky, messy, and loaded with bacon, which is loved by every dude I know, though of course ladies are welcome to try this decadent treat. **SERVES 15**

INGREDIENTS

30 sheets (about 1 package) phyllo dough, thawed

1½ cups (3 sticks) butter, melted

1 pound bacon, cooked, cooled, and chopped

2 cups chopped pecans

FOR TOPPING

½ cup water

½ cup maple syrup

1½ cups brown sugar

1 teaspoon vanilla extract

1 teaspoon maple extract

1. Preheat oven to 350 degrees F. Liberally grease a 9×13" baking pan with cooking spray.

2. Place one sheet of phyllo dough into the bottom of the prepared pan. Brush the phyllo with butter, then layer on another piece of phyllo. Repeat this process another 8 times for a total of 10 sheets.

3. Sprinkle half of the bacon and half of the pecans onto the phyllo evenly, then repeat the layering process another 10 times, making sure to butter each piece of phyllo. After layering another 10 phyllo sheets, sprinkle with the remaining bacon pieces and chopped pecans.

4. Layer another 10 phyllo sheets, buttering each sheet, to complete the baklava. Cut the baklava carefully into a diamond or square pattern and bake for approximately 35 to 40 minutes or until golden brown and crispy.

5. While baklava bakes, make your syrup. In a medium saucepot, mix the water, maple syrup, brown sugar, and vanilla and maple extracts together over medium heat until smooth. Bring the mixture to a boil, then reduce heat and simmer for 10 to 15 minutes or until slightly thickened. Remove from heat and set aside.

6. Pour the sauce over the baked baklava and allow the baklava to cool and set for at least 6 hours. Just before serving, cut the baklava once more.

Homemade Peanut Butter Cups

I like consistency. I order the same thing at restaurants, keep my hair the same color, and wear virtually the same thing every day. Heck, I listen to the same songs over and over, which must drive any of my car passengers crazy. I like eating the same foods—there are no weird surprises and I know exactly what to expect. If you're anything like me, you'll appreciate that these Homemade Peanut Butter Cups taste exactly like their famous counterpart, but homemade. Hey, if it ain't broke, don't fix it. **14 CANDIES**

INGREDIENTS

1 (16-ounce) package chocolate almond bark

¾ cup creamy peanut butter, divided

½–¾ cup powdered sugar

3 tablespoons butter, room temperature

1 teaspoon vanilla extract

1. Line 2 muffin pans with 14 paper liners. Set aside briefly.

2. In a large microwave-safe bowl, melt chocolate almond bark according to package directions until smooth. Stir in ¼ cup peanut butter.

3. Drop tablespoons of the chocolate mixture into the bottom of each muffin cup. Use the back of the spoon to "paint" the chocolate up the sides of the muffin cup just a little bit. Pop the muffin tins in the freezer for about 5 to 7 minutes.

4. While the chocolate sets, make your peanut butter filling. In a large bowl, beat the remaining peanut butter, ½ cup of powdered sugar, the softened butter, and the vanilla extract with an electric mixer. If the mixture is very soft, add the remaining powdered sugar; you want it to be on the stiffer, spreadable side.

5. Re-melt the remaining chocolate mixture. Set aside.

6. Drop rounded tablespoons of the peanut butter mixture on top of the chocolate cups, smoothing out the top with a greased spoon. Immediately top with a heaping tablespoon of the remaining chocolate mixture, trying your best to ease the chocolate down the sides of the peanut butter, too. Place the muffin pans back in the freezer to set for about 10 to 15 minutes before serving.

S'mores Crispy Treat Bark

It's no surprise that I'm a little strange. For one, I like singing Spice Girls to my dogs in an opera voice, so that should tell you plenty. Two, when I think of s'mores, I think of the wintertime, whereas everyone else considers this American favorite a summertime treat. To me, s'mores taste best when the marshmallows are toasty and slightly charred over a fire . . . which has no place when it's sweltering outside. Plus, there's something so heartwarming and comforting about gooey marshmallows, melted chocolate, and crisp graham crackers that screams "winter break." Thankfully, even if you disagree with my season choices, we can agree that this S'mores Crispy Treat Bark tastes amazing year-round. SERVES 6–8

INGREDIENTS

2½ cups Rice Krispies cereal

1½ cups miniature marshmallows

3 cups white chocolate chips

⅓ cup Biscoff spread (see Note)

2 cups semi-sweet chocolate chips

FOR TOPPING

½ cup graham cracker crumbs

1 cup marshmallow bits

NOTE: Biscoff spread is cookie butter spread. It's made with crushed Biscoff cookies, and is very similar to peanut butter. You can find this near the peanut butter at the grocery store.

1. Line a large rimmed baking sheet with foil or a silicone liner. Set aside. In a large bowl, add the cereal and miniature marshmallows. Set aside.

2. In a large microwave-safe bowl, melt the white chocolate chips on HIGH power for 30 to 35 seconds. Stir, then melt again for another 20 to 25 seconds. Stir once more until melted, then add in the Biscoff spread. Pour this mixture over the cereal mixture and toss to combine until thoroughly coated.

3. Spread the coated cereal mixture onto the prepared pan in an even layer, about ¼" thick. Place in the freezer to set for about 10 minutes.

4. While the white chocolate layer sets, melt the semi-sweet chocolate chips in another large microwave-safe bowl for 45 seconds. Stir, then heat for another 30 seconds, stirring until melted and smooth. Pour the chocolate evenly over the top of the white chocolate layer and spread out to the edges. Immediately sprinkle the graham cracker crumbs and marshmallow bits evenly over the top. Place in the freezer to chill for another 10 minutes before breaking into pieces.

Strawberry Marshmallow Kebabs

July can get very hot, so I try to avoid cooking as much as possible. I rely a lot on no-bake desserts and slow-cooker meals that won't add fuel to the inferno that is our home. And is it just me, or does anyone else always crave baked treats when it's pushing 100 degrees outside? I always crave gooey brownies or layer cakes when the temperatures rise. Thankfully, you can purchase them, but I always like to kick it up a notch. In this recipe, I combine strawberries and brownies with marshmallows for a delicious sugar rush. **SERVES: 4–6**

INGREDIENTS

Kebab skewers

Fresh strawberries, tops cut off

Large marshmallows

Brownie bites, cut in half

FOR TOPPING

2 squares chocolate candy coating/
almond bark

NOTE: Did you notice there aren't exact measurements for this recipe? The beauty is that you can make however many or few as you'd like! If you're making an exceptionally large batch, I'd double or even triple the chocolate bark amount.

1. Skewer one strawberry, one marshmallow, and one brownie bite half. Repeat with another one of each ingredient. Set on a foil-lined baking sheet. Repeat with other kebabs.

2. Just before serving, melt the chocolate bark according to package directions, or until smooth and melted. Drizzle evenly over the kebabs.